T0131537

INCARNATION

INCARNATION

The History and Mysticism of the Tulku Tradition of Tibet

TULKU THONDUP

SHAMBHALA
Boulder
2011

Shambhala Publications, Inc.
4720 Walnut Street
Boulder, Colorado 80301
www.shambhala.com

© 2011 by Tulku Thondup Rinpoche

The Buddhayana Foundation Series XII

Designed by Steve Dyer
Printed in the United States of America

⊗ This edition is printed on acid-free paper that meets the
American National Standards Institute z39.48 Standard.
♻Shambhala Publications makes every effort to print on recycled paper.
For more information, please visit www.shambhala.com.
Distributed in the United States by Penguin Random House LLC
and in Canada by Random House of Canada Ltd

LIBRARY OF CONGRESS CATALOGING-IN-PUBLICATION DATA
Thondup, Tulku.
Incarnation: the history and mysticism of the tulku tradition of Tibet/
Tulku Thondup.—1st ed.
    p.   cm.—(The Buddhayana Foundation series; 12)
Includes bibliographical references and index.
ISBN 978-1-59030-839-4 (pbk.)
1. Reincarnate lamas—China—Tibet. 2. Reincarnation—Buddhism.
I. Title.
BQ7610.T46 2011
294.3'923092—dc22
2011000515

CONTENTS

PREFACE

IN THIS BOOK I present the fundamental principles of tulku-hood; the ways of recognizing them; the stories of their miracles, their clairvoyance, and their visions; their memories of their past lives; the roles they have played in history; the goals they fulfilled; and signs of attainment they have displayed at death.

I wrote this book in response to the queries of a number of inquiring minds who have not found a comprehensive explanation of the tulku principle in Western writings. I have tried to distill the entire spectrum of tulkus' philosophical views, different cultures, and miracles. I am not aware of any other study that encompasses all this in one book in any language, including Tibetan. I hope that in the future scholars will lend the light of their knowledge to refining and advancing our understanding of this field of inquiry, because the tulku system is one of the golden pillars of the centuries-old culture, religion, and society of Tibet.

I would have liked to provide sketches of the lives of the major tulkus of all the Tibetan Buddhist lineages. However, my knowledge is limited, as is space in this book. So I pray for forgiveness from all those whom I could not include or present adequately.

TULKU THONDUP
September 2009

ACKNOWLEDGMENTS

I AM THANKFUL to Harold Talbott for editing this book with his deep knowledge of Dharma and unswerving dedication, as always. And, I thank Lydia Segal for encouraging me to tackle this important but hugely complex field and for lending her editing skills and caring support.

I am deeply grateful to Michael Baldwin for his most caring heart and insightful eyes. I thank the patrons of the Buddhayana Foundation for their utmost generosity in supporting our translation and writing projects for the last three decades.

I am highly indebted to Acharya Emily Bower and Katie Keach of Shambhala Publications for transforming this book with their mastery of letters. I will always be grateful to Acharya Samuel Bercholz, Peter Turner, Lenny Jacobs, Jonathan Green, and all the wonderful friends at Shambhala for giving birth to and nourishing my beloved books for years. I am highly thankful to Dave O'Neal for writing the back cover description, to Hazel Bercholz for the cover design, to Steve Dyer and Lora Zorian for the book's interior design, to Daia Gerson for copyediting, to Nancy Crompton for proofreading, to Jim Rosen for taking many of the photographs with great care, and to Sheila McBroom for indexing with love.

INCARNATION

· I ·

An Overview of the
Three Types of Tulkus

Countless reflections [the tulkus]
of the sun, which is the Buddha,
appear simultaneously
in every bowl of pure water, which are the disciples.
　—ASANGA

*T*ULKU IS THE Tibetan translation of the original Sanskrit
term *nirmanakaya*.[1] The term *tulku* has been translated as "the
manifested-body, created-body, manifestation" or also as "incarnation, reincarnation, or rebirth." It has been translated
into Chinese as *huofo*,[2] which means "living buddha," and
into Mongolian as *qubilyan*. Tulkus are the principal standard-
bearers of the Buddhist tradition of Tibet and the providers
of spiritual and social guidance for both the ordained and the
laity. Tibetan Buddhists have been meticulously following the
tradition of finding, recognizing, enthroning, training, and
venerating the tulkus for over a millennium.

In the literature and history of Tibetan Buddhism we can
see three categories of tulku. They are the emanations of the
buddhas, the manifestations of the highly accomplished adepts,
and the rebirths of highly virtuous teachers or spiritual friends.

First, there are the buddha manifestations (Skt., nirmanakaya), or the tulkus who appear to ordinary beings and serve
them in infinite forms simultaneously through their fully enlightened power.

Second, there are the tulkus or the manifestations of highly accomplished adepts,[3] who appear in many forms through the power of their highly realized wisdom.

Third, there are the rebirths, or tulkus, of virtuous or meritorious teachers,[4] who are fulfilling their own spiritual goals and serving others through the beneficial effects of their virtuous deeds. Most of the tulkus of Tibet might belong to this third category, the rebirths of virtuous teachers or lamas.

Originally, tulkus were manifested by the enlightened power of the buddhas, as well as by highly accomplished adepts. However, Tibetan Buddhists have also adopted the term and the concept of tulku for the rebirths[5] of virtuous lamas. Buddhists of Tibet believe that Buddhist masters will take rebirth after each of their deaths. In fact, Tibetan Buddhists trust that every being takes rebirth. And because they trust in karma, they believe that deceased lamas, who have accumulated virtuous karma, will obtain rebirths that enable them to benefit others. They believe that lamas obtain rebirths that enable them to benefit others because they trust in karma and know that the deceased lamas have accumulated virtuous karma. Tibetan Buddhists believe that virtue, or "merit," is the source of happiness and enlightenment, and that those who have attained this by leading virtuous lives will be sources of great benefit for many beings. They also believe that the tulkus of virtuous lamas will be sources of great benefit for many beings, because the lamas have led very virtuous lives, and virtue, or merit, is the source of happiness and enlightenment to Tibetan Buddhists.

Tibetan Buddhists also believe in the power of highly accomplished adepts to find the reborn manifestions of deceased lamas, because they trust in the power of highly realized wisdom-mind. Tibetan Buddhists enjoy full trust in the tulku tradition because it is based on mahayana fundamentals, and they have witnessed and appreciated an abundance of benefit from the good merit of tulkus.

. . .

It is impossible for ordinary people like myself to judge which tulku belongs to which category. For they all appear more or less similar—kind and honest people who are seriously following and practicing Dharma and dedicating their lives to serving many. The depth of their wisdom realization is impossible for ordinary minds to see and measure.

Unless one is omniscient or at least enjoys some degree of clairvoyance, no one can judge others. One can see how others appear and how they are behaving, but not who they are or why they are behaving in a particular manner. For example, enlightened ones such as buddhas, bodhisattvas, and sages appear in peaceful forms and wrathful forms, but all their activities will be for serving others with love. As for false tulkus, even if they show impressive performances, their goal could be for material and emotional satisfaction for themselves or their loved ones. This is why the fully enlightened Buddha said, "Apart from myself and those like me, no one can judge another person."[6] So, I myself have no way of judging if someone is a real tulku or not. I am only repeating what the masters of the past have said.

The best approach for us is to view all the true tulkus as objects of respect, means of learning, and sources of blessings. Such pure perception and proper training will benefit us, and it fulfills the goals of tulku manifestations.

Tibetans generally take tulkus to be authentic if they have been recognized by highly qualified, well-known, and truly respected lamas and if they have been enthroned in their original seats by the chief disciples of the previous incarnation or the legitimate authorities of their previous institutions. For Tibetans, it is also highly appreciated if tulkus show miraculous signs,[7] maintain recollections of their past lives, or, especially, manifest any spiritual qualities of their previous incarnations as proof of their being the true tulkus of those particular lamas.

In most cases, a tulku is recognized by a highly realized lama before the tender age of four or five. Not long after they are recognized, their intensive training begins, and it can last for twenty years or more. They are generally educated under the watchful eyes of well-trained teachers in the best facilities available. Most tulkus are born with gifted qualities, but even if they are not, the chances of their becoming highly skilled teachers are very high because of the special attention and training they receive.

The main purpose of this tulku training is not so that they can qualify for a successful career, but so that they grow into skilled teachers and public servants who will serve the monasteries or nunneries and the whole society.

From Tibetan Buddhist literature we can learn about the profundity of the concept of tulkuhood in detail as taught by the Buddha, ancient Indian masters, and Tibetan scholars and adepts. The tulku system has offered unimaginable contributions to the spiritual, academic, and social world of Tibet. The imprints of the tulkus' lives—their writings, their teachings, and the institutions they have built—have become the main providers of education and spiritual civilization in Tibet, the Land of Snow, for centuries.

· 2 ·

The History of the
Tulku Tradition

FROM THE TIME that the Buddha's teachings arrived in Tibet, there were a number of highly realized people who were known as tulkus of buddhas, of adepts, or of virtuous lamas. For example, King Trisong Detsen of Tibet was known as the tulku of Manjusri, the Buddha of Wisdom. Yeshe Tsogyal was the tulku of Tara, a buddha in female form. Nyang Nyima Ozer and Guru Chöwang, the great adepts and *tertöns,* were the tulkus of King Trisong Detsen. In the ninth century, Guru Padmasambhava gave a prophecy to the king about the king's future tulkus:

> Lord, you will serve beings in India for (the next)
>   thirteen lives.
> After that, in the region of Lungmar of Lhotrag,
> You will take birth as Nima Ozer, a master of kama and
>   terma teachings
> And you will serve beings through esoteric activities.
> After that, in Pangje of Lhotrag,
> You will manifest as Chökyi Wangchug.[1]

There were many earlier lamas who were known as tulkus, but the Second Karmapa commonly became known as the first tulku in Tibet because he was formally recognized as a tulku of the First Karmapa. He was enthroned on his previous

The Second Karmapa was the first officially recognized tulku.

monastic seat and continued the Dharma activities of his previous incarnation.

THE SECOND KARMAPA (1206–83)

Pomdrakpa Rinpoche kept having visions of the First Karmapa, Dusum Khyenpa, whenever he saw a particular gifted boy called Chödzin.[2] One day, the First Karmapa appeared in a vision and told Pomdrakpa, "Chödzin is in fact my rebirth."[3] After a while, Pomdrakpa told Chödzin, "Now, taking care of the tradition of Dusum Khyenpa and his followers is your responsibility." Soon Chödzin became renowned as Karma Pakshi, the most miraculous Karmapa, the Second. Since then, the unbroken tulku lineage of the Karmapas has been presiding over the Karma Kagyu tradition of Tibetan Buddhism. The present Karmapa is the Seventeenth.

THE SECOND DALAI LAMA (1476–1541)[4]

One of the most important tulku lineages of Tibet has been that of the Dalai Lamas. The Second Dalai Lama, Gedun Gyatso, remembered his previous life as a child and said, "My name is Pema Dorje." Pema Dorje was the First Dalai Lama's child-hood name. Then, at the age of three, he told his mother, "I am not going to stay at home. I will go to live in Tashi Lhunpo. There, I have better houses than here. I have left candies there to eat." Tashi Lhunpo was the monastery founded by the First Dalai Lama.

At the age of five, one spring when Gedun Gyatso heard the sound of thunder, he raised his head and listened to it. Then he said, "It sounded like the Father Lobzang Tragpa giving teachings." His father asked, "How did Father Lobzang Tragpa teach?" Imitating, he raised his voice and recited a four-line verse on the qualities of teachers that starts, "The teacher must be peaceful, very peaceful and totally peaceful. . . ."[5]

Lobzang Tragpa, also known as Je Tsongkhapa, founded the Gelug school and was the teacher of the First Dalai Lama. Here, "father" means "spiritual father," the person who gave Gedun Gyatso his Dharma life. Also indicating where he went between his previous life and this life, Gedun Gyatso continued, "I first visited Tusita Heaven. Maitreya, Atisa, and Tsongkhapa were there. They were giving many teachings. I received them."

At the age of ten, Gedun Gyatso was enthroned at Tashi Lhunpo as the Second Dalai Lama. Since then the successive Dalai Lamas have been recognized and enthroned as Dalai

The Second Dalai Lama was one of the foremost tulkus.

Lamas not by genealogy, election, or selection, but by recognition of their rebirths, the tulku lineage.

Aside from these two most important tulkus, thousands of boys and girls have been officially recognized as the tulkus of different high Buddhist masters and have been enthroned in the seats of their previous incarnations. The tulku tradition has also been well established in Mongolia for centuries, and now has even started in other countries, too.

· 3 ·

The Four Foundations
of the Tulku Principle

In ORDER TO UNDERSTAND the three different categories
of tulku, we need to understand the foundations of the very
principle that tulkuhood is based upon: the following four
Buddhist principles. The first foundation is the three buddha-
bodies, the three aspects that constitute buddhahood; the second is enlightened aspiration, the sublime vow or commitment
to serve all who are in need of help and whose hearts are open
to Dharma and Dharma teachers; the third is karma, the ineluctable universal law of the endless cycle of cause and effect;
and the fourth is rebirth, the unavoidable part of the cycle of
life of every being.

THE THREE BUDDHA-BODIES[1]

The principle of the three Buddha-bodies is taught in Mahayana Buddhism. The Buddha said,

> Buddha embodies three bodies.
> They are the ultimate-body, enjoyment-body,
>   and manifested-body.[2]

Longchen Rabjam explains:

> Ultimate-body, enjoyment-body, and manifested-body
> Are like the sky, the sun, and their reflections in clear
>   lakes.[3]

Ultimate-Body[4]

This is the openness, or emptiness nature, of universal buddha-hood. It is the ultimate basis of all, which is the two purities—totally pure from its beginningless origin, and totally pure from any adventitious defilement. It remains forever as the unchanging and open nature, like space. It is the self-awareness and all-knowing wisdom that sees all simultaneously, with no dualistic thoughts, conceptual characteristics, or efforts. It is the true nature and source of all the enlightened qualities. Never moving from such primordial space, it facilitates the arising of the two form buddha-bodies—the enjoyment-body and the manifested-body—to fulfill the needs of all, as the sky enables showers to saturate the fields.

Enjoyment-Body[5]

This is the spontaneously present clarity and radiance of that buddhahood. It is the ultimately pure and ever-present form-body of the Buddha with fivefold-wisdom.[6] It is self-appearing in the form of five buddha-families[7] and the pure lands with five certainties[8] like the lights of the sun and moon. They can only be perceived by the wisdom-minds of the enlightened ones,[9] who are free from dualistic thoughts and afflicting emotions[10] with traces. Such pure forms of buddhas and Buddha pure lands, and the wisdom and wisdom light, are natural, indivisible, ever-present, changeless, and effortless.

Manifested-Body

The manifested-body, or "tulku" in Tibetan, is the main or direct source of the tulku principle. But in order to understand its whole scope, we are outlining all three buddha-bodies. The manifested-body is the manifestation of the buddhas appearing in various ordinary forms and activities, so that they can be visible for ordinary beings whose minds are open, like infinite reflections of the sun. So, infinitely manifested forms can appear simultaneously or consecutively, depending on the receptive vessels of beings. Manifested-bodies are not the true buddha-forms, but they are the manifested forms through which the buddhas make themselves visible to ordinary beings and serve them. Among the three buddha-bodies, the manifested-body is the only form that can be seen by beings like us, who have dualistic concepts,[11] defiled emotions, and eyes of flesh.

Highly accomplished adepts enjoy the power of manifesting many tulkus in various forms, but not as vastly as the buddhas do. Virtuous lamas, on the other hand, will have only one tulku or rebirth, and only after their death.

The forms and activities of the tulkus of the buddhas appear, not because of the karmic causations or conditions of the buddhas themselves, but for two main reasons. First, they appear solely in response to and in accordance with the karmic openness, potential, and needs of the audience, the ordinary beings. Second, they appear due to the power of the enlightened aspirations of the buddhas for serving others.

The availability of the tulkus of the buddhas and adepts is not limited to so-called Buddhists. For example, Buddha and buddha-qualities have arisen from the ultimate and universal nature and they can appear in any form, at any place, and for any being who is ready to perceive them.

The Father and Son Meeting Sutra says,

> Whether in the forms of Indra and Brahma
>   (divine beings) or
> In the forms of *mara* (demonic forces),
> Buddha fulfills the needs of beings—
> Although mundane beings do not realize it. . . .
>
> Buddha remains untainted by mundane stains
> Like the lotus that does not get soaked.
> He acts in accordance with the diverse dispositions
> Of the beings of this mundane world. . . .

Buddha does not have desire, although he manifests as
   though he has.
He does not have fear, although he manifests as though
   he has.
For the sake of beings,
Buddha manifests them through his miraculous power.

Buddha has no ignorance, although he manifests as
   though he has.
He is not ordinary, although he manifests as though
   he were.
For the purpose of taming beings,
Buddha shows various manifestations.[12]

Four Categories of the Manifested-Body, or Tulku

The manifested-body itself has four categories: the supreme
manifested-body, the artisan manifested-body, the birth manifested-body, and the diverse manifested-body.[13] However,
in many teachings the artisan and diverse manifested-bodies
are combined as one and designated as the artisan manifested-
body.[14]

Supreme Manifested-Body:[15] This is the highest form of buddha that ordinary beings can see. Such manifestations are endowed with unique qualities: a body with "thirty-two major
and eighty minor, excellent marks," speech with "sixty aspects
of melodiousness," and a mind with "omniscient wisdom."
This buddha serves beings through the skillful methods of
"twelve enlightened deeds." More than twenty-five centuries
ago, Buddha Sakyamuni took birth in India in the form of
a supreme manifested-body, or supreme tulku. He performed
twelve enlightened deeds. Asanga lists them:

1. Descending from the Tusita Heaven
2. Entering the womb
3. Taking birth

4. Excelling in various artistic skills
5. Enjoying the queen's companionship
6. Renouncing household life
7. Training in ascetic practices
8. Proceeding to the heart of enlightenment
9. Taming the forces of maras
10. Attaining full enlightenment
11. Turning the wheel of Dharma
12. Entering into *parinirvana*[16]

Artisan Manifested-Body:[17] This is the apparition of the buddhas in the form of any artisan, such as a violinist. This form miraculously appears to inspire, serve, or guide a being or beings into the path of peace, joy, and enlightenment without actually taking birth as a being.

Birth Manifested-Body:[18] This is the manifestation of the buddhas that takes birth as a human being, an animal, a bird, and so on in order in order to serve others. It doesn't have to be in one particular form or another—men or women, human beings or animals, rich or poor, religious or secular, gentle or rough, beautiful or ugly—but rather in any form that leads a being or beings toward happiness, peace, and enlightenment, either directly or indirectly. Buddha himself said at the time of his parinirvana,

> O Ananda, do not mourn. O Ananda, do not cry.
> During the final five-hundred-year period,
> I shall come as virtuous teachers
> To serve you and others[19]

The principle of the birth manifested-body of the buddhas is the direct origin of the three kinds of tulkus known in Tibet. We will discuss them later.

Diverse Manifested-Body:[20] This is the manifestation of the buddhas in various inanimate forms, such as religious artifacts,

books, images, paintings, flowers, food, clothing, shelters, and
medicines that benefit beings. Santideva made aspirations:

> May I become ships, ferries or bridges for those who
>   wish to cross rivers or oceans.
> May I become islands for those who wish to find land.
> May I become lamps for those who need light.
> May I become shelters for those who are looking for
>   places to live.[21]

These three buddha-bodies are the true nature and pure
qualities of the whole universe. The ultimate peace and openness (emptiness)—the awakened nature—is the true and ultimate nature of all, as space pervades all. That is the true nature,
the ultimate-body. In that ultimate space, boundless radiance
of the enlightened qualities is always glowing spontaneously,
limitlessly, and ceaselessly. Those are the true qualities, the
enjoyment-body. The teachers, teachings, and various spiritual sources appear in various conventional forms in order to
reach ordinary beings and lead them to the realization of their
own enlightened nature and qualities, buddhahood. Those are
the ordinary forms, the manifested-body. These three buddha-
bodies are not the nature and qualities of some exceptional
group. They are the three aspects of the true nature and qualities of all. Nagarjuna writes,

> Whatever is the nature of the Tathagatha (Buddha)
> Is the nature of beings.[22]

Every being inherits such a buddha-nature and qualities. But
our nature and qualities have temporarily been covered by our
own nightmarelike transitory delusions rooted in the tightness of the grip of grasping of our own dualistic minds. Such
dualistic concepts have produced chains of afflicting emotions,
stirred up turbulent karmic conflicts, and forced us to endure
reckless seesaws of misery. Thereby, most of us have lost even

the clue of having this utmost peaceful, joyful, and enlightened nature of ours. But the darkness-like confusions and miseries caused by grasping at mental objects with the force of emotional flames are impermanent and transitory. They will never last and will vanish at the touch of the sunrays-like light of wisdom.

The trainings on the path of virtuous deeds that generate peace, joy, and wisdom in our mind-stream are the indispensable means of uncovering our own enlightened nature and qualities, the buddha-bodies. All the positive thoughts and pure activities, such as learning, praying, and serving others, and especially meditation will lead us directly or indirectly to the awakened state of our own pure nature and qualities.

The Enlightened Aspirations[23]

Enlightened aspiration is the vow or commitment to dedicate one's thoughts and activities to serving all beings without any selfish motivation. The power of such a vow ignites the flame of passion and commitment in oneself, lasting not only for this lifetime but for all successive lives until the attainment of buddhahood. Such an attitude must be observed by all "the seekers of enlightenment."[24] If people are followers of the mahayana path, they must be "seekers of enlightenment," and whatever they are thinking or doing, they must be thinking and doing it with pure intention and total dedication.

One sees all beings as loving beings, like one's own loving mother, and makes the commitment or vow to take responsibility to serve them with the strength of one's compassion and loving-kindness. Such meditators put this intention into real practice by turning every activity of their lives—big or small—into the service of others from the depth of their hearts. Whether they are doing meditation, saying prayers, cleaning the house, giving a piece of bread to a hungry person, or even just entering a city or waking up in the morning, they will be doing it with the intention to serve others directly or indirectly with pure love. Then the whole of life will transform into a life of true love and wisdom, a source of pure joy and peace for oneself and others.

KARMA

Karma is the law of the cycle of cause and effect. Every positive or negative volitional act—mental, vocal, or physical—will produce its commensurate effects in the form of pleasant or painful results. That is the ineluctable law of life of all ordinary beings and the conventional world. Master Vasubandu writes,

> Through the law of karma,
> Various worlds have evolved.[25]

The past positive or negative deeds of beings determine their future happiness or painful experiences. All the experiences of our lives are mere responses and reactions to what we have been registering in our mind-stream, thereby planting habitual karmic seeds in the universal ground, the unconsciousness state, of our mind. Every happening of our life is the maturation of those karmic seeds. Seeds of positive deeds, such as the thoughts, words, and physical actions of love and wisdom will produce peaceful, happy, and enlightening results. Dislike, anger, and attachment bring us only pain and suffering. Until the attainment of buddhahood, which transcends the karmic cycle, we will be enjoying continuously the effects of the past karmas, and in every moment we are creating many new karmas. Such karma can be created and experienced collectively by many beings together or individually. Karmic results are not about rewards or punishments that are carried out by some external forces or agents, but they are the effects of the actions and reactions of our own deeds that are returning to us.

Therefore, if one has lived with positive deeds, then because of the force of that karmic law, one will enjoy a peaceful and joyful life now and in future lives. Especially, if one has realized high spiritual attainments, one will not only be enjoying a peaceful and joyful life but will also become a great source of peace and joy for many.

Rebirth

As long as they are still under the karmic influence, rebirth is the inevitable future for every ordinary being and even for some accomplished meditators. According to Buddhism, death is not the end of life. Your physical body will dissolve into the elements at the time of death. But your mind or consciousness—your true identity—will take rebirth according to what your past karma will ordain for you. The chain of lives will go on through successive deaths and births, until the chain of karmas ceases upon the attainment of buddhahood.

As soon as important lamas die, Tibetans fully expect that they will find the rebirths, the tulkus, of their teachers without any question. If the deceased lamas are the manifestation of Buddhas or highly accomplished adepts, then they will not be taking rebirth due to their karma, but solely to care for and serve others. If deceased lamas have been simple adepts or virtuous lamas, then they will be taking beneficial rebirths according to their past virtuous deeds since they have not yet transcended the cycle of karmic effects, but will have committed no or few unvirtuous deeds. They will all be sources of great benefit, as they are the products of love, wisdom, and service—the virtuous deeds.

In addition, most of the followers of deceased lamas believe in the tulku tradition and in the spiritual powers of their lamas.

Therefore, they trust that their deceased lamas will return to serve many beings, especially the lamas' own past associates and societies, in order to continue the service they have been offering and cherishing. The followers also trust in the power of the past mutual karmic and sacred commitments that they and the lamas have made to one another.

· 4 ·

The Three Main
Types of Tulkus

As mentioned in chapter 1, there are different categories of tulkus in Tibet because there are different degrees of spiritual attainment as well as many different qualities of tulkus.

Tulkus of Buddhas

These are "the birth-manifested-bodies" of buddhahood.[1] They are the buddhas who appear in various forms, capacities, and activities in order to serve the wishes and the needs of unenlightened beings. These tulkus can appear and function in any form or manner, at any time or place. These forms might include a person who is wealthy, a person who is impoverished, a person who is healthy, a person who is sick, educated, or illiterate, gentle or wild, wrathful or peaceful—or the tulku of a buddha might even appear as an animal.

Both buddhas and adepts can manifest multiple tulkus simultaneously. They can do so at any time and in any place due to their enlightened power. This includes *ma-de* tulkus,[2] ones who manifest even while their predecessor is still alive. When I was growing up in Tibet, I knew about two tulkus who manifested themselves during the lifetime of their respective "predecessors." One of them was Ma-de Tulku of Gyangwa from the Dzamthang Monastery of Dzika Valley; the other one was Ma-de Tulku of Shichen of Shichen Monastery in Serta. In *The Mishap Lineage,* Chögyam Trungpa Rinpoche said, "There are tulkus who incarnate before the previous incarnation has died, several months or even years earlier."[3]

The purpose of these buddhas' miraculous appearances is solely to benefit others in one way or another. Their appearances are not caused by their own karmic circumstances, but by two factors: the loving aspirations of the buddhas to serve beings who are in need of help; and the karmic receptiveness and needs of the beings themselves.

All the tulkus of buddhas enjoy the same qualities:— unconditional love, omniscient wisdom, and boundless power. And they appear in various forms and activities, depending on the needs and capacities of beings. For example, Maitreya Buddha appeared to the great adept Asanga in the form of an angry, sick, and hungry dog, at a time when Asanga had lost his inspiration. The suffering dog invoked great compassion and unconditional love in Asanga. Instantly, Asanga was able to see the dog as Maitreya Buddha, and he received teachings and blessings from him. Asanga became one of the greatest mahayana masters.[4]

Tulkus of buddhas always embody the three "buddhabodies," although ordinary beings can see them only as humans. The first body is their primordial purity and openness nature: their ultimate-body. Their ever-present innate clarity and enlightened qualities are the second body, the enjoyment-body. Their appearance in an ordinary form in order to benefit beings is the third, the manifested-body. A prayer to the Third Dodrupchen Rinpoche describes the three buddhabodies:

> From the space of ultimate basis,
>   the primordial purity, the ultimate-body,
> Projects various displays in the ten directions—
>   the enjoyment-body,
> Serving all beings ceaselessly, the manifested-body:
> Jigme Tenpe Gyaltshen—to you I pray.[5]

Tulkus of Adepts

Many tulkus in Tibet are believed to be the rebirths of highly accomplished adepts. They may be bodhisattvas, the seekers of enlightenment who have reached high stages of attainment through training in the teachings of sutra.[6] Or they could be siddhas, highly accomplished masters[7] who have trained through the path of tantra. Here, the word *sutra* refers to the common or exoteric teachings and *tantra* means the secret or esoteric teachings of Mahayana Buddhism. Also bodhisattvas may or may not be siddhas, but the siddhas must be bodhisattvas.

As an adept advances through the ten stages of attainment, he or she purifies greater and greater degrees of dualistic obscurations—intellectual and emotional ignorance—and they complete the two accumulations: those of merit and of wisdom. When an adept has fully purified his or her obscurations, along with any remaining traces of ignorance, and has fully completed and perfected the two accumulations, he or she becomes a fully enlightened buddha.[8]

The adept who has reached any of the first ten stages[9] of spiritual attainment achieves the power of manifesting many tulkus simultaneously.[10] These can appear at any time and any place in accordance with the needs of others. They can also manifest their next incarnation before their own death. However, adepts do not have the power to manifest infinite tulkus, as the buddhas do. Neither do they have the omniscient knowledge of the buddhas. Even the great adepts, such as Sariputra and Mahamaudgalyayana, did not know all, as the Buddha did. According to tradition, the foreknowledge and power of the Buddhas are limitless. But adepts' foreknowledge and powers are also limited in four respects. They are as follows: They don't know all the qualities of the Buddha because those qualities are too profound. They don't see or know about things in very distant places because they are too far away. They don't

see events that occurred or will occur in distant times, as those
are too remote. And they don't perceive specific details, such as
the causes and conditions that create the karma of individuals,
because those are too subtle.[11]

Adepts who have realized "the eighth stage" or higher enjoy
the ten powers, which include taking any birth anywhere, for
the purpose of serving others. The activities of adepts in whatever form they might appear always fulfill two purposes (the
goals of oneself and of others) simultaneously. The great adept
and celebrated scholar Naropa of Nalanda Monastery served
his teacher, the great master Tilopa, who lived as a beggar,
with total devotion, including performing twenty-four life-
threatening sacrifices. One day Tilopa hit Naropa on the head
with his shoe, knocking him unconscious. When he regained
consciousness, Naropa found that his wisdom realization had
become equal to Tilopa's.[12] This story shows that if a tulku is
an adept, his or her activities might appear to be unusual, but
they will always serve others. In this case, being struck awakened enlightened nature for Naropa.

Highly accomplished adepts are never derailed from their
path, because their thoughts and actions are always meritorious and enlightening. Even if they haven't yet fully uprooted
the seeds of karmic cycles, they have diminished them greatly.
None of their activities cause any negative effect, because
adepts don't indulge in negative thoughts and emotions. Instead they bring their realization to bear on the transformation
of their actions into enlightened deeds. So, whatever they do,
they always fulfill the dual purpose of attaining enlightenment
for self and other in the light of true love and wisdom.

TULKUS OF VIRTUOUS LAMAS

Most of the tulkus in Tibet seem to be the rebirths of virtuous
lamas, or virtuous friends who have performed many beneficial
acts.[13] They are loving, generous, learned, moral, meditative,

and they serve others. They have not yet been freed from the cycle of karmic conditions and they do not yet enjoy miraculous powers to any great degree. However, because of their past meritorious deeds and their realization, they will take rebirth as human beings and will become the source of great benefit for many beings. Virtuous lamas may also take rebirth in Buddha pure lands and progress in their spiritual path by accumulating merit of greater degrees and wisdom more quickly than in an ordinary world. They remain as great sources of help for many through their spiritual power and manifestations as various forms. Ultimately they attain buddhahood and serve others through infinite buddha manifestations.

The tulkus of virtuous lamas take rebirth mainly because of their own past karma, most of which is virtuous. However, many of them could still be susceptible to negative karmic effects and vulnerable to confusion, anger, and craving, which lead to negative actions. They could also experience suffering and could even fall from tulkuhood as the result of negative actions. So, for many of them it is essential to remain on the right path with great care and consistency in order to complete their spiritual journey.

As part of their training in pure perception, Buddhist scholars in Tibet view all tulkus, and especially their own teachers and preceptors, as buddha manifestations or the tulkus of highly accomplished adepts. I have no way of knowing who belongs in which of these categories and I do not attempt to categorize any individual tulkus.

· 5 ·

The Secondary Types
of Tulkus

ASIDE FROM the main categories of tulku, we also find additional, or secondary, types of tulku. These are the unrecognized tulkus, blessed tulkus, and tulkus fallen from the path.

UNRECOGNIZED TULKUS[1]

According to Buddhist beliefs, there are infinite numbers of tulkus of the buddhas and adepts in various forms, in infinite world systems, serving infinite beings, although only limited numbers might ever have been recognized or known as tulkus, even in Tibet, where there is a system for recognizing them. As we discussed earlier, whether or not someone is designated as a tulku, he or she will always benefit many through various means and forms—animate as well as inanimate—with great effect.

The historical Buddha himself told many stories[2] of his own previous lives—as he remembered them through the power of his enlightened wisdom. During those lives he was accumulating merit, progressing through the realization of various stages of wisdom, and serving beings for eons before he became the Buddha, the Fully Awakened One.

According to the sutras,[3] numerous eons ago, when the Buddha was an ordinary being, he took rebirth in a hell realm. He suffered gravely there as a result of his past negative karma.

He and a companion were forced to pull a wheel of fire on which a wrathful hell-guard was sitting, holding a burning club with which to beat them. His companion was so weak that he couldn't pull the wheel anymore. The hell-guard stabbed his companion with a burning trident. His companion kept crying loudly and bleeding profusely. At that moment, with strong love and compassion, the Buddha developed enlightened aspiration, a vow to take responsibility for helping his companion and all the suffering beings from the depth of his heart, and he became a bodhisattva for the first time.[4] The bodhisattva begged the hell-guard, "Please have a little mercy on my suffering companion." At that, in a rage the hell-guard hit him with a burning trident. Because of the power of his strong compassion, the bodhisattva died and was liberated from the hell-realm. His evil deeds of many eons were purified instantly by the power of such enlightened aspiration. Thereafter, he started his journey toward the fully enlightened state of buddhahood.

After that, for numerous successive lives, remaining firmly on the path of enlightenment as a bodhisattva, he served infinite beings with that irreversible enlightened aspiration, helping others at the cost of his own life with no selfish interest. His earlier successive rebirths were tulkus of virtuous ones, and later rebirths were tulkus of adepts, but there was no tradition of recognizing or enthroning any tulkus at that time. After Buddha's attainment of buddhahood, he has served, and will continue to serve, infinite beings whose minds are open with infinite tulkus, the manifested-bodies of the Buddha.

Likewise, many great beings in Tibet have been tulkus—the manifestations of enlightened ones—but they were not recognized or enthroned formally as tulkus, as is done today.

So there are two kinds of unrecognized tulkus. Many tulkus with extraordinary qualities have become known and respected as tulkus in the latter parts of their lives, or posthumously, while many others have always remained unknown.

However, both types have played their designated enlightened roles and carried out beneficial service for many.

MARPA CHÖKYI LODRÖ (1012–96)

This great master was born in Lhodrak in Southern Tibet. First he studied with the great translator Drokmi (992–1072) in Tibet. Then he went to India and spent twelve years at Pullahari Monastery receiving teachings and transmissions from the great adept Naropa. In those days, getting to India from Tibet was a life-risking journey, but he went to India two more times to receive transmissions from Naropa, Maitripa, and other great adepts of the esoteric Buddhist world.

In Tibet, Marpa translated many tantras and taught them to many disciples. Among his main disciples was the most famous ascetic and adept Milarepa, who in turn entrusted Marpa's teachings to the great scholar-saint Gampopa. Marpa founded the Kagyu School (Order of the Oral Teachings) of Tibetan Buddhism. Milarepa, Gampopa, and numerous others have propagated and maintained that lineage and it remains active today.

Marpa wasn't enthroned as a tulku, but was known as the Tulku of Bodhisattva Samantabhadra and Dombhi Heruka, who was one of the eighty-four Mahasiddhas of India.[5]

SACHEN KUNGA NYINGPO (1092–1158)

Sachen was the son of Khon Könchok Gyalpo (1034–1102), the founder of the Sakya School of Tibetan Buddhism. He studied with his father, as well as with Bari Lotsawa, Mal Lotsawa, Lama Zhangton, and many others. After meditating on Manjusri, the Buddha of Wisdom, for six months, he saw him in pure visions. Manjusri gave him the heart of the teachings in four famous lines called *The Parting from the Four Attachments*:

> If you have attachment to this life, you are not a Dharma
> practitioner.
> If you have attachment to the three worlds, you are not a
> renunciate.

If you have attachment to self-interests, you don't have
 bodhicitta.
If you have grasping, you don't have (the realization of)
 the view.

Sachen Kunga Nyingpo received many profound teachings and transmissions from Mahasidda Virupa in pure visions.
Sachen was clairvoyant and miraculous. He manifested himself
in six different places simultaneously.

Among his disciples were his two famous sons, Sonam Tsemo
and Drakpa Gyaltsen. Sachen wasn't enthroned as a tulku, but
was known as an emanation of Avalokitesvara Buddha and his
four tulkus are believed to have taken rebirth in four different
pure lands simultaneously.

GYALSE THOGME (1295–1369)[6]

This master was a great scholar, and his life was filled with
miracles, but his most amazing quality was to have been born
with a heart of great compassion. He was compassionate to
all: to inanimate things, to people, and to animals, whether
they were caring or harmful. Whatever and whoever he saw,
he treated them as loving beings; he was a being of total love
and compassion. One day, when he was very young and was
resting in his mother's lap, he saw a leaf carried away high into
the sky by the wind. This made him cry intensely, so when
his mother asked why he was upset, Gyalse Thogme pointed
to the leaf and said, "A being is being carried away." One day,
after he had started walking, he went outside and a little later
came back naked and cold. When his mother asked why he was
naked, he replied, "I gave my clothes to a being in the cold."
His mother went out and saw that her son had covered a frost-
covered bush with his clothes and had placed small stones at the
edges of the clothes so that they would not be blown away by
the wind.

When he would play with his playmates, he never felt sad
because of losing, but rather couldn't face winning and making

someone else sad. Whenever he went to collect firewood with
others, if the others couldn't get firewood, he would give them
some that he had collected, or he would help them to collect
some for themselves. Later, reflecting back, he said, "I never
dared to utter any harsh word to anyone."

Later he became one of the greatest scholars, bodhisattvas,
and teachers of the Tibetan Buddhist world. Among his writings were *The Thirty-seven Verses on the Practices of Bodhisattvas*,
a short but masterly handbook for all to train on the path of
enlightenment.

JE TSONGKHAPA (1357–1419)

This great master was the founder of the Gelug school (Virtuous Order) of Tibetan Buddhism. He was born in Amdo
in Eastern Tibet, and was ordained as a devotee (Skt., *upa-
saka*) by the Fourth Karmapa, Rolpe Dorje. At the age of 16,
Je Tsongkhapa went to Central Tibet and studied with many
great masters such as Zhönu Lodrö, Redawa, and Lekyi Dorje.
He became renowned for the brilliance of his scholarship. For
years he followed an ascetic path and meditated in solitude.
Then in 1409, he founded Gaden Monastery, where he empha-
sized strict monastic discipline. His disciples established many
other important monasteries in Central Tibet that had the same
monastic code, including Drepung, in 1416; Sera, in 1419; and
Tashi Lhunpo, in 1447. Je Tsongkhapa wrote over two hundred
treatises in over twenty volumes. Among his numerous great
disciples were Khedrupje, the First Panchen Lama; Gyaltsabje,
the First Gaden Tripa; and the First Dalai Lama.

Je Tsongkhapa was not enthroned as a tulku, but it is believed that at the time of Buddha Sakyamuni, he had been born
as a son of a brahman in India. Offering a white crystal rosary,
he generated enlightened aspiration at the feet of the Buddha
and became a bodhisattva. According to Panchen Lobzang
Chögyan, Tsongkhapa was a manifestation of Guru Padmasambhava. Panchen writes: "The glorious Lobzang Tragpa

Je Tsongkhapa was a renowned scholar, known as an incarnation of the Buddha of Wisdom.

[another name for Je Tsongkhapa] is the manifestation of the knowledge holder, the Lord of the Realized Ones, Padmasambhava."[7] After his passing, it is believed that Je Tsongkhapa took rebirth as a bodhisattva in Tusita, one of the six god realms of the "desire world" of Buddhist cosmology.[8]

RIGDZIN JIGME LINGPA (1729–98)[9]

Jigme Lingpa was born into the family of a humble yogi, and yet later founded the Longchen Nyingthig lineage of the Nyingma school. When he was young, despite living in a monastery, he did not have much opportunity to study. But

Rigdzin Jigme Lingpa manifested three extraordinary tulku incarnations simultaneously: Do Khyentse, Paltrul Rinpoche, and Khyentse'i Wangpo.

in his autobiography he wrote that because of the realization of his past lives, he started to manifest the qualities of a great adept. Because of his high realization, his speech was suddenly empowered. His throat opened as "the cycle of wealth" of teachings. He was able to teach the most profound teachings to many disciples with great fluency, even though he hadn't studied those teachings himself. His physical channels transformed into "the clouds of letters." All phenomenal appearances before him appeared as "the symbols of Dharma." His speech became the sound waves of profound realization. He could see his past lives clearly, as if in dreams. His writings became treatises of great scholarship. An inexhaustible ocean of teachings continued to burst from him.[10]

According to his recollections and revelations, many millennia ago Jigme Lingpa was born in India as the son of a king named Krikri, and he developed enlightened aspiration (Skt., *bodhicitta*) in front of Buddha Kasyapa. (This is the third buddha of the thousand buddhas of this age. Buddha Sakyamuni was the fourth one in this system.) After that, he took many successive remarkable lives, including that of King Trisong Detsen of Tibet. In the far future, he said, he will become a buddha known as Nampar Gyalwachen:

> After developing enlightened aspiration at the feet of
>   Kasyapa Buddha,
> He has accomplished vast bodhisattva activities.
> Ultimately, he will attain full enlightenment as Nampar
>   Gyalwachen.[11]

LAMA ZHINGKYONG (D. 1959?)

Lama Zhingkyong was born in Golok, Tibet, and became a learned, great meditator and a very kind and most humble being. He was thought to be a tulku of Drime Zhingkyong, an important lama of the Kathog lineage. He was also amazingly clairvoyant. For example, he once wrote a prophecy for me on a piece of paper. It said, "When the twin-fire[12] years arise, you will travel toward Central Tibet. That will be auspicious. . . ." At that time, I hadn't even dreamed of leaving for Central Tibet and didn't pay any attention to what he said. But four or five years later, in 1957, we (myself and my tutor, Kyala Khenpo) were suddenly forced to flee toward Central Tibet. I asked Lama Zhingkyong to write about my future, without giving even a hint that we were thinking of leaving. He wrote again, "When the fire-egg breaks, you will reach Central Tibet. . . ." In fact, two months later, we left Eastern Tibet and reached Lhasa in Central Tibet on the sixth day of the first month of the Fire Bird year (1957).

YOGI YANG-RI (D. 1983)

Yogi Yang-ri was a monk in Dodrupchen Monastery. He knew only how to read the daily prayers. He often talked quite snappishly, acted roughly, and dressed ruggedly. Some even thought that he shouldn't be residing in the monastery at all, although he did practice celibacy. In the latter part of his life, when the political situation in Tibet became difficult, he became clairvoyant and began to make predictions and show miraculous displays. He inspired many to sincerely practice Dharma by reaching their hearts directly with simple and straight teachings, and with prophetic skill. Many people respected him as a tulku of a special being, but no one knew whose tulku he was. He was a hermit yogi and showed no interest in such a designation. Many other great practitioners have similarly become known as tulkus only in the later stages of their lives.

BLESSED TULKUS[13]

The principle of blessed tulku isn't as well known or as fully defined as the other types. But we can distinguish two kinds of blessed tulkus in the Tibetan tulku tradition. In the first case, some enlightened lamas themselves bless the rebirths of other lamas as their own tulkus. In the second case, some enlightened lamas recognize the rebirths of lamas as also being the tulkus of other lamas and bless them as such. Both of these types of recognized tulkus are not the actual rebirth of the lamas they were recognized as, but the blessing from another lama serves as a substitute through the power of blessings.

This tradition of recognition is not by mistake or due to corruption, but for good purposes. Due to interdependent causation, the service to beings and for the Dharma that blessed tulkus give will be more effective and beneficial than the services of the original lamas would have been.

TSHEWANG NORBU (1698–1755)
This abbot of Kathog Monastery was recognized as a tulku of
Namkhe Nyingpo, one of the twenty-five chief disciples of
Guru Padmasambhava. But Tshewang Norbu himself said, "I
accept this (recognition) as a designation of Namkhe Nyingpo's
tulku being given to someone who is only blessed by Namkhe
Nyingpo." Then he also added, "I am not a rebirth tulku (Tib.,
skye sprul) of Namkhe Nyingpo, but I might be a manifestation of the power of his blessings.[14] I certainly have had vague
memories of him throughout my life, even as a child."[15] Once,
my teacher, Kyala Khenpo Rinpoche,[16] explained the principle
of the blessed tulku to me with a contemporary story: "The
tulku named Dzamba (d. 1959) was recognized as the tulku
of Wangde Lingtul. Tulku Dzamba was miraculous and beneficial for many. But the lama who recognized the tulku himself explained, that Tulku Dzamba was not the actual tulku of
Lingtul, but by having the title of Lingtul's tulku conferred
upon him, Dzamba's acts would become more beneficial, and
that became true."

These blessed tulkus themselves might belong to any one
of the three categories of tulkus that we discussed earlier. But
here they are playing the role of the tulku of another deceased
lama, who could also belong to any of the three categories.
And, in some cases, the blessed tulkus may not be tulkus in
terms of their spiritual attainments, but they will become beneficial vehicles for serving others if they are recognized as such
and if they follow the right disciplines. In any case, blessed
tulkus have great opportunities for serving others' needs, and
by receiving the title of "tulku" they serve others with greater
dedication.

Chögyam Trungpa Rinpoche interprets the blessed-tulku
concept as follows: "[A] blessed tulku, in which the previous
person chooses the person who is closest to him, or blesses
some passing bodhisattva who hasn't quite attained the highest of the bhumis. He blesses that person, and he takes certain

types of energy, or spiritual energy, which transcends ego anyway, and transfers it to the chosen person. That person then
comes back as the incarnation of the previous person."[17] He
further observes, "Generally, in Tibet the blessed tulkus seem
to be most prominent."[18]

I myself was recognized as the tulku of Konme Khenpo,[19] a
highly celebrated scholar and miraculous adept. Since I had
heard the principle of the blessed tulkus, I was convinced that
I must be a blessed tulku of this great khenpo for two reasons:
First, I was recognized by three great adepts—Tulku Dorje
Dradul, a great adept and the youngest son of Dudjom Lingpa;
Pushul Lama, a great scholar and a true living bodhisattva;
and Apang Tertön, one of the great tertöns of the twentieth
century. So it is not possible that they made a mistake or were
influenced by corrupt people. Secondly, with the exception of
some simple signs of being a devout person in the past, I do not
possess any attainment of the great khenpo that would confirm
me to be his real tulku. So, I concluded that I must be a blessed
tulku of this great khenpo. However, my queries didn't end
there. I kept thinking, "Now, what was the reason that I was
recognized as a blessed tulku of this great khenpo?" In 1999,
when one of my books, *Masters of Meditation and Miracles,* had
just been released, I had a moment of understanding. While
holding this book in my hand, thoughts flooded forth: "Oh,
this is why I was recognized as a tulku. I am here to pre-
serve the amazing life stories and legacies of many great lamas
by putting their precious life stories together in this book, so
that they can keep the light of inspiration on in the hearts of
many!" That put my inquiring mind at rest.

FALLEN TULKUS[20]

Many tulkus of virtuous lamas, although they are real tulkus,
could fall from the path of Dharma and from tulkuhood if they

were not to refrain from indulging in negative deeds and were not to devote their lives to spiritual training. This happens when the spiritual realization is not yet high and irreversible and they still carry negative mental, emotional, and karmic deposits in their mind-stream. A tulku can easily succumb to the effects of unhealthy external influences, emotional attractions, and unhealthy activities if proper safeguards such as caring teachers, alert guardians, supportive friends, and a healthy environment are not available at times of need. Also, many times, unfortunately, the companions and fellow students, and the institutions that are supposed to be safeguarding the welfare of young tulkus themselves may become the culprits that have a hazardous effect on the lives and missions of the young tulkus, causing them to fall from the hard-earned path before they can stand on their own feet.

Views of Fallen Tulkus in Different Schools

Different religious institutions of Tibet have different systems of judging tulkus as to whether they are maintaining their status or not. The ways that tulkus maintain their status and fulfill the purpose of tulkuhood is through preserving and developing the unique traditions of their previous incarnations. They should study hard to learn the Dharma, meditate to strengthen their understanding, reach higher spiritual attainment, and work hard to propagate Dharma and serve others. For example, the Nyingma school, one of the four major Buddhist schools of Tibet, was founded in the ninth century by the great adept Padmasambhava and the great bodhisattva Santaraksita. They established two ordained sangha or Dharma communities. One is the community of renunciates,[21] the monks and nuns who have renounced their household life and live as celibates. The other is the community of tantrikas,[22] the followers of the esoteric path. A great number of them are married and live at home with their families. Some Western writers call these two communities "ordained" and "lay," but such designations are wrong. Tantrikas are those who are ordained and initiated into the highest disciplines of Buddhism, and they are the observers of esoteric vows. Whether individual tantrikas are observing their vows properly or not is an individual issue, and the same applies to renunciates. So, in the Nyingma, they are still maintaining the two ordained communities, or clerical systems, and tulkus could be either celibates or *tantrikas,* who are not celibates. So, in the Nyingma, those tulkus who are not observing or have broken the vows observed by their respective communities and who have neglected to repair them are considered fallen tulkus.

The Kagyu school was founded by Marpa Chökyi Lodrö, a great tantrika and a "householder master." However, most of his later followers—the lamas, tulkus, and clerical members— became renunciates, or celibates. Similarly, the Sakya school was founded by Khon Könchok Gyalpo, also a famous tantric master. Nonetheless almost all of his followers—the lamas, tulkus, and clerical members—have become renunciates, or celibates. So the tulkus of these two schools, although they are fully trained in tantric teachings, with the exception of some cases, have all been renunciates, and therefore if they were to abandon celibacy, they could fall from their position as recognized tulkus and lamas.

The Gelug school was founded by Tsongkhapa, a highly celebrated scholar and a proponent of strict monastic rules. In order to be a tulku or a lama in the Gelug school, one must be a renunciate. The followers of Gelug are fully trained in tantra, but to be a married tantric lama or tulku is not an option. So if a tulku renounces the vow of celibacy, he or she will neither remain a tulku nor function as a lama in the Gelug school.

However, since the middle of the twentieth century, the strict requirements of celibacy for tulkus and lamas seem to be changing in these schools. Importantly, if the hearts of the tulkus are filled with pure love for others, total faith in Dharma, and wisdom from spiritual attainment, and if they are honestly dedicating their lives in service to others and to the Dharma, they are considered to be fully functioning as tulkus, regardless of the tradition they belong to. However, if their minds are conflicted and controlled by the eight worldly affairs, then the lights of love, faith, and wisdom of their hearts could turn off before they even know it. All the activities of their lives could become aimed at self-satisfaction. They could misuse sacred Dharma materials and services to glorify themselves. Then they are fallen tulkus. Jigme Lingpa laments finding that so many are bound by the eight worldly affairs:

> With the exception of those who have realized the truth,
> Among all those who are known as priests, ascetics,
>   or lamas,
> Those are rare who are not bound by the eight worldly
>   affairs,
> Such as (craving for) praise, respect, and service.[23]

There are those tulkus who are not yet highly accomplished. In these cases, if they relax their mental and physical disciplines and stray into erroneous behaviors, then they have obviously already fallen off the true tulku wagon, even if they are satisfying some technical obligations of being a tulku. So, like any student of Dharma, tulkus too must check their own minds and lives at the turn of every moment, in every situation. They must remain vigilant about their mental and physical activities so that they can catch themselves before falling too deeply down the slope of greed and hatred, or praising themselves with arrogance and derogating others with contempt.

Gyalse Thogme wrote,

> If you don't examine your own faults,
> You might be appearing as a Dharma practitioner,

but are indulging in non–Dharma activities.
Therefore, always check your own faults and
   abandon them.
That is the training of the bodhisattvas.[24]

Atisa said,

Attainment of supreme miracles is the decrease
   of greed.[25]

The Buddha said,

Those bodhisattvas, who praise themselves and
   condemn others
Are possessed by maras.[26]

Paltrul Rinpoche was a famous tulku and hermit who made
the following aspirations for not falling into the swamplike
entrapments of having fame and material possessions, for many
tulkus plunge into them and sink deeper and deeper into the
entrapments:

First is the praise of empty words that have no basis.
Second is the honors that elevate you to high
   pedestals that have no benefits.
Third is the material offerings of faith that come
   with heavy (karmic) burdens.
By renouncing these three, may I the dog, die
   like a dog.[27]

Tulku Drachen of Lauthang warned me strongly against falling
into the traps of having impressive credentials and attractive
possessions, as many young tulkus do, before gaining any true
knowledge and realization:

There are many who are holding the vaselike precious
   titles of great beings,

But possess very little content (wisdom) from studies,
  research, or meditation.
They are just wrapped up in the ornaments of celebrity.
For you to follow such a life is inappropriate.
Getting too attached to people,
Trusting those who are deceivers,
Praising self and digging at others without noticing
  one's own faults,
Are not the ways of holy beings. Be aware!
Those who cherish material goods as the dearest goals,
Wandering through the doors of towns to perform rites
  (for collection) as beggars, and
Holding self-interest tightly at the heart, but pretending
  to care for others as a show
Are mere shadows of ascetics.
How could anyone follow them![28]

Gifts, money, and services that are dedicated by devotees
with respect and trust in the service of Dharma activities,
Dharma objects, or religious communities[29] are known as *kor*,[30]
or materials of faith. For Dharma teachers, one of the dangers
of falling is through collecting kor with greed, and misusing it.
If, lacking the spiritual power to digest such offerings, teachers greedily enjoy kor for their own comfort and especially if
we use them for any purpose other than that intended by the
providers,[31] they are misusing the highly potent kor. Kor is
one of the hardest things to digest; it's like molten lava. Misuse
of Dharma materials and deceiving others about the extent of
their realization for the purpose of being given kor are a sure
way for tulkus to fall from the enlightening path and to sink
into the bottomless karmic pit of misery. The *Sutra of Great
Liberation* says, "If I steal or if I enjoy the materials of the sangha
(religious community), . . . or of ordained individuals or patrons, or if I claim that I have realized the four absorptions
or four fruits without having them . . . all these will certainly

cause me to take rebirth among the beings of the hell realm, if
I haven't purified them with remorse."[32] Exposing the weak-
ness of many tulkus, Paltrul Rinpoche bluntly argued for the
importance of meditation training for them:

> Those lamas and tulkus who are adorned with high ti-
> tles and are taking offerings for the dead, must develop
> enlightened attitudes (loving-kindness and compassion)
> and perform effective ritual ceremonies with prayers and
> aspirations. Merely thinking, "I am so-and-so," will not
> work. There are tulkus who have been recognized as the
> rebirths of past holy masters. But they have to study like
> ordinary people. They have to start their studies with the
> alphabet—*ka, kha, ga,* and *nga.* If they have forgotten how
> to read, it is very doubtful that they remember the train-
> ings of development stage and perfection stage. So I sus-
> pect that they might need a little training in developing
> the enlightened attitude, and they must do some medita-
> tion retreats instead of enjoying kor as soon as they can
> ride horses.[33]

Once Tarthang Choktul Rinpoche advised me personally,
when I was in my early teens, "Nowadays, all the tulkus—
myself and others—have started collecting kor as soon as we
can pick up the ritual vases. We have made ourselves as dark
(unvirtuous) as inkpots. Please try to avoid indulging in such
kor until your training is completed. I am telling you this because I will be happy if you do well and I will feel sad if you do
badly. As you know, I am a student of Lushul Khenpo."

Also I vividly remember Kyala Khenpo—my teacher, tutor,
and parent from the age of four through the age of eighteen—repeatedly telling me, "As long as I am alive, I will make
sure that you don't have to indulge in any kor. But after that, it
is up to you. But be careful, it is poisonous!" He always wished
me to be a tulku who is, he said, "Not just one who can repeat

the teachings, but a person content with little, so that what you see will be what you get."

However, soon after Khenpo's passing away, while fleeing toward India to start a refugee life, I hesitantly started taking Dharma offerings and many of my dreams inspired by the great teachers remained unfulfilled. Before crossing the border into India in 1957, I went with some lamas to the home of a simple family to perform a two-day ceremony. At the end, when the family gave me some money as an offering for doing the ceremonies, as they did to each lama, I said, "No, I don't take any offerings!" What I said shocked everyone, including myself. I knew that I was there to get offerings so that I could buy some food and cross the border. But the old warning against taking offerings suddenly kicked in, unconsciously. This habit of declining offers didn't last long. For the past many decades, as a writer of Dharma books and a meditation instructor in the West, not accepting any Dharma-related offering has become a dream of a distant past. When I receive offerings, I accept them and I try to be mindful of spending money in the way that the donor intended.

If, on the other hand, tulkus and teachers use dharma offerings with pure minds for their intended purposes, there will be great benefit for them and enormous merit for those who gave the donations. There are many tulkus and teachers whose minds are rich with true spiritual realization and whose hearts are filled with pure love and beneficent intentions for others. Such people don't even dare to know how to indulge in the misuse of materials and services of kor, because they are free from selfish thoughts. They accept the offerings out of pure hearts with appreciation and thankfulness for the generosity of the givers, and use them fully for the intended purpose. So they are only providing themselves as the vessels for others to make merit by opening their hearts with generosity, love, and devotion. If a tulku accepts offerings with pure thoughts of love and appreciation, and if he or she uses the gifts for their intended purpose, then the tulku transmutes the whole process of offering and accepting into a golden source of merit.

In that way, when tulkus accept Dharma offerings with pure thoughts and if they use them for the right purposes, the offerings will become a source of merit for both the provider and the receiver.

FALSE TULKUS

Some people might carry the nametag of "tulku," but they are false tulkus.[34] In the past, and especially in today's world, we frequently encounter people who claim to be tulkus, even tulkus of the highest lamas ever known. If we check carefully, though, most of them have not been recognized or enthroned in a traditional way, nor have they gone through any serious training. Even more shockingly, many of them manifest very few real tulku qualities—peace in the heart, love for all, and realization of the true wisdom.

In some cases, the lamas who recognized such tulkus are not equipped for such a task. They lack the enlightened power and extraordinary capacity that is necessary for recognizing the rebirths of other lamas. Relying on some simple signs, such as dreams, they might honestly believe in what the dreams predict, but they may just be fooling themselves and others. Sometimes the recognition and training process of young tulkus are run by smart bureaucrats with special interests and agendas in their hearts, who lack either honesty or true care for traditional values or spiritual wisdom. Sometimes people may witness simple miracles happening around certain young children that impress them. Yet some unhealthy spirit forces may have orchestrated these happenings in order to fool people.

As a safeguard against such problems, the followers of a deceased lama usually seek the prophesies and visions of not just one but a number of highly respected lamas before making the final recognition. It is always important to consult a highly competent lama, or a number of them.

The main cause of corruption, however, is not the lack of merit of the tulku tradition in general or the lack of enlightened lamas who are able to recognize them. Rather, it is the greed for material or social gain that drives the parents, relatives, or other interested people to fabricate stories and manipulate the process in favor of their own candidate. In the past, institutions such as monasteries and nunneries mostly maintained strict and vigilant safeguards against such improper influences. But today, in many cases, the institutions themselves are powerless at best.

Another factor is the greed of the young people themselves. Today, many well-intentioned institutions that would be capable of offering watchful guidance have little control over what goes on. So individuals with little merit are often free to proclaim themselves tulkus.

Such false tulkus or teachers, although they appear impressive, could hurt the Dharma in the end and ransack the true value of the thousand-year-old tulku tradition. Such possibilities were prophesied by Guru Padmasambhava in the ninth century:

> There will come teachers who act as if they are me,
> though they are not.
> They will claim to be my tulkus, but dismantle my
> tradition.
> They deceive many with teachings of demonic and
> unknown entities.
> Nonhuman forces prop them up and promote their
> celebrity.
> Such teachers of erroneous paths cause the Dharma to
> decline.
> They don't practice (Dharma), but only talk and only
> intensify desire.

They contradict what they teach and what they do, and
    indulge in corrupt activities.
Without gaining any confidence, they are zealous to
    teach others.
They lack any intention of benefiting others, but focus
    on self-interest.
They lack moral discipline. Dharma will be left just as
    a shadow.[35]

Paltrul Rinpoche writes:

These days there are many so-called Dharma-holders,
Who claim to perform Dharma activities.
But they have no experience of what Dharma is.
They are ruining the foundation of the precious Dharma.
    It is serious![36]

Great Khenpo Ngachung laments:

Having been designated as the Tulkus of holy Lamas of
    the past,
Many roam as the leaders of the ceremony business as
    soon as they can stand up and sit down—
Without having done any training in the vast and
    profound sutras and tantras.
Such Tulkus have become the refuges of the faithful
    and deceased. How sad! [37]

KADAMPA DESHEG (1122–92)[1]

This lama was one of the greatest scholars and adepts of the Nyingma school and the founder of Kathog Monastery. At the age of seventy-one, he gave the following advice to his disciples in the monastery's garden: "No matter how high your realization is, you must live with moral discipline meticulously, as it is the essence of Buddha's doctrine. No matter how many words you know, they are just dead words; you must meditate and enjoy the experiences of their meaning. According to both higher and lower *yanas,* there is no more important goal to achieve than taming one's own mind. Please train in Dharma one-pointedly, while remaining humble. Because of meditation, the masters of our lineage attained the light-body (at the time of their death). If I had gone to Kampo (to meditate in seclusion), I would have attained the light-body too, for others to appreciate. Instead, I took disciples and taught them—there is no difference for myself (whether I attain the light-body or not)." He urged again and again, "You must turn back your mind from samsara. Meditate on bodhicitta." Then he made an elaborate feast offering. At this his disciples beseeched him to live longer. But he said, "Now I have accomplished all my purposes (of living). I am going to the victorious Buddha of Infinite Light. . . . May the Dharma of the Buddha remain for a long time." Then, in the garden itself, he sat up, facing toward the West with the gesture of "the relaxation of the mind," and died. Instantly, the earth shook gently. A soothing sound was heard nine times. From the West a rainbow light extended to his body. Snowflakes started to fall from the cloudless clear sky, as if rains of flowers were showering. The hearts of all who were there were moved with devotion. It is known that he took rebirth as a bodhisattva named Wisdom-Heart in the Blissful Pure Land of Amitabha Buddha. In the future he will become a buddha known as the Buddha of Infinite Life.

DUDJOM LINGPA (1835–1903)[2]

This great master announced that he was going to the valley of Pemako—a sacred place that was blessed by Guru Padmasambhava as a "hidden land."[3] Pemako was situated about eight hundred miles west of his hermitage in Do (rDo) Valley in the Golok region of Eastern Tibet. He inspired hundreds of people to vow to travel to Pemako. His followers made a palanquin to carry him on their back as he couldn't ride a horse or walk. But the palanquin turned out to be too small for him. At that, he said, "It is fine. It is just symbolic." When his son, the third Dodrupchen Rinpoche, heard what his father said, he remarked, "He is not going to Pemako, but he is taking rebirth there. If he were actually traveling, he would need a real palanquin, not just a symbolic one."

When the advance group of his followers started to leave for Pemako, he said, "Go first. But, I will get to Pemako before you people get there." But they didn't understand what he meant. In fact, weeks later Dudjom Lingpa died and took rebirth in Pemako as the famous Dudjom Rinpoche.

MIPHAM RINPOCHE (1846–1912)[4]

This great scholar and adept said, at the time of his passing, "After this life, I will never take rebirth in this mundane world. I will remain only in pure lands. However, because of the power of aspirations, it is natural that the display of my tulkus as the Noble Ones will appear as long as samsara remains." When people urged him to live longer, he said, "I certainly will not live. I will not take rebirth either. I am going to Shambhala in the North."

APANG TERTÖN (1895–1944/45)

This adept was a great *tertön* and miraculous teacher in Golok Province. He visited me when I was two years old to bless and perform ceremonies for me, though I cannot remember it. At the time of his passing, Apang Tertön told his family, "I will be

Dudjom Rinpoche was a prolific writer and adept who recognized the disciples of his previous incarnation.

taking rebirth in the family of Sakya Gongma. Come to visit me when I am about three years old and make offerings to the Sakya, Ngor, and Tashi Lhunpo monasteries." Sure enough, Sakya Trizin was born into the Sakya Gongma's family.

DUDJOM RINPOCHE (1904–87)

The young tulku was recognized by Jetrung Jampa Jungne by clearly prophesying the names of the tulku's birthplace and parents. When people from Golok arrived in Pemako, the little tulku called a number of them by name, and many were moved to tears.

Dudjom Rinpoche was the most compassionate sage, brilliant scholar, prolific writer, and the holder and propagator of all the teachings of the Nyingma lineage. He was renowned as the Master of Masters, a Guru Padmasambhava in human form for the twentieth century.

Sakya Trizin's previous incarnation foretold where he would take rebirth, and Sakya Trizin remembered who he was at his birth.

SAKYA TRIZIN (1945–)

As a toddler he said, "I came from a far distant place. I lived in a tent. I have a wife and children." In addition, his first words were in the Golok dialect. He recognized an old student of Apang Tertön, even remembering his name. When Sakya Trizin was three years old, Tulku Wangchen Nyima, the oldest son of Apang Tertön, went to Sakya, a distance of over five months' travel by horse, to meet this incarnation of his father, and I have vivid recollections of him describing the visit to the small tulku upon his return, when I was about eleven years old. Now a highly learned and accomplished adept, Sakya Trizin is tirelessly working on preserving the centuries-old authentic nectarlike teachings and spreading them all over the world—a true expression of a tulku manifestation.

LAMA SÖNAM DRAGPA (D. 1955)

Lama Sönam Dragpa was a most respected scholar and a most honest and humble person—a true bodhisattva. He left the following letter when he died: "As soon as I die, I will take rebirth in the Blissful Pure Land.[5] I have recited the texts on the *Perfection of Wisdom*[6] one hundred and eight times by myself and have meditated on their profound meaning in this lifetime. Therefore, I will be known as Bodhisattva Wisdom-Heart.[7] Whoever prays to me with devotion, I will protect them from any danger they might face while they are alive. I will lead them to the Blissful Pure Land when they die." He concluded the statement with the following five-line prayer to himself to be recited by his devotees:

> In the Blissful Pure Land you are Wisdom-Heart.
> In the Snow Land [Tibet] you were Sönam Dragpa.
> In the future you will be known as the Buddha of
>   Infinite Life.
> My root lama—to you I pray.
> Please empower me/us to take rebirth in the Blissful
>   Pure Land.

This prayer is almost identical to the prayer, mentioned earlier, of Kadampa Desheg, the founder of the famous Kathog Monastery in Eastern Tibet. Rewriting this prayer for himself, Sönam Dragpa proclaimed that he was a tulku of Kadampa Desheg, but people learned this only after his passing. I was one of the two people who went into his room after his passing and found this letter at his bedside written in his own hand. I was about twelve years old.

THE SIXTEENTH KARMAPA, RANGJUNG RIGPE DORJE (1924–81)[8]

The Fifteenth Karmapa entrusted a letter to the hand of Jampal Tsultrim, his attendant, that clearly described where his tulku would take rebirth. As detailed in the letter, they found his tulku, the Sixteenth Karmapa, in Kham, Eastern Tibet. The Sixteenth Karmapa was born in an earthen house to an aristocratic family called Athub on the upper banks of the Yangtse

*The Sixteenth Karmapa was a supreme master of masters,
a recognizer of many incarnations.*

River in Denkhog (the Valley of Den), where the legendary warrior Denma, a minister of Ling Gesar, ruled centuries ago. When he was seven years old, he was recognized by the Eleventh Tai Situ Rinpoche of Palpung and other lamas as the Sixteenth Karmapa, and was later enthroned at Tsurphu, the seat of the Karmapas in Central Tibet.

Rigpe Dorje was one of the most powerful and compassionate Buddhist masters of the twentieth century. He became instrumental in spreading Buddhism to many countries of the world and was one of the greatest authorities in recognizing tulkus through the power of his foreknowledge.

TULKUS WHO SAY WHO THEY WERE
WHEN THEY START SPEAKING

Some tulkus will remember and say who they were in their previous life, expressing their wish to return to their monastery or nunnery.

MACHIG LABDRON (1055–1149)[9]

This famous mystic, one of the greatest female teachers of Tibet, reported that she was the tulku of Zhonnu Monlam Grub, a great adept of India. When still in her teens, Machig Labdron burst forth her past brilliance with little effort of studies, defeating many scholars, who'd been swollen with pride, and exhibiting numerous miracles. She founded the tradition of *Chöd*, or "cutting off ego"—the practice that perfects the realization of the wisdom of emptiness. She is still inspiring thousands of lazy hearts to become devout Dharma practitioners even to this day. Even in her time, her teachings reached beyond the borders of Tibet, which was rare. She herself proclaimed,

> All those teachings have been translated from Indian
> languages into Tibetan,
> But the teachings that have been translated from Tibetan
> into Indian languages are only mine.

THE THIRD KARMAPA (1284–1339)[10]

The Third Karmapa remembered his past lives as various great masters in India and Tibet. He also clearly recalled the life he led just before his present one. He said that he was in Tushita Heaven in the presence of Maitreya Buddha and many enlightened ones. There, many deities approached and requested that he take rebirth in the human world, saying,

> For you taking rebirth in a precious human life has
> arrived.
> To hold the tradition of Dharma there has arrived.

Becoming the parents of beings has arrived.
The time has arrived. Samaya!

When he was three years old, he and his playmates built a throne, which he liked to sit upon while wearing a black hat and proclaiming, "I am the Karmapa."[11] Important lamas soon recognized him as the Third Karmapa.

NANGSA ODBUM (TWELFTH TO THIRTEENTH CENTURY)[12]

This great teacher was one of the well-known *delogs,* or "the returners from death."[13] For centuries, a number of people in Tibet went through extraordinary experiences of dying and going through the unknown phases of life after death. They would remain dead with no breath or heat in their body for days. Then they slowly returned to life with vivid memories of the experiences that they had had. They were thereafter able to live for many years teaching the true mysteries of life and helping others to prepare for their own death experiences. Thus, when Nangsa Odbum died, her mind—the consciousness—traveled through the *bardo,* or the transitional realms between life and death. During the judgment stage, the Lord of the Dead told her to return to the world of the living to serve many. Soon she revived and became a well-known propagator of Dharma and a miraculous adept. One of her great tulkus was Jetsun Migyur Paldron of Mintrolling Monastery, who remembered clearly being Nangsa Odbum, among others, in previous lives.[14]

DO KHYENTSE YESHE DORJE (1800–66)[15]

This great adept was one of the tulkus of Jigme Lingpa. As soon as he was born, he stood up, holding the beams of the sun that were shining through holes in the tent as if they were solid, and chanted all sixteen vowels and thirty consonants of Sanskrit. On the third day after his birth, he vanished for three days. During those three days, Do Khyentse visited the Glorious Copper-colored Mountain[16] Pure Land. Then on the

Do Khyentse Yeshe Dorje was the most miraculous adept of the Nyingma lineage.

third day, his mother saw him standing on the bed. She ex-
claimed, "Baby is here standing!" When the boy heard that,
he suddenly fell down. That woke him up to the conventional
world. From that point on, his perceptions and actions became
a little bit more conventional. As a child, Do Khyentse remembered the monastery where Jigme Lingpa, his previous birth,
lived, as well as Samye Chimpu, where Jigme Lingpa did his
years of retreat. When he turned one year old, he kept insisting
that his parents should take him to see a lama named Sönam
Chöden. This was a childhood name of the First Dodrupchen,

the chief disciple of Jigme Lingpa, but even Dodrupchen's current attendants didn't know this name at the time.

SHUGSEB LOCHEN CHÖNYI ZANGMO
(1865–1953)[17]

This yogini was one of the famous teachers of the twentieth century in Tibet. When she was born near Rewalsar in India, people heard in the air the singing sound of OM MA-NI PAD-ME HUNG and saw other signs. She is known as a tulku of Machig Labdron.

She studied with many teachers and trained in Dharma while living in poverty, but with spiritual wealth, joy, and dedication. When she was still in her early teens, she saw in a dream a woman singing the stories of "the returners from death." After that she started teaching Dharma to gatherings in the streets and markets by singing those stories as well as the mantra OM MA-NI PAD-ME HUNG. People were mesmerized by her voice, melodies, teachings, and presence, and many became deeply inspired to practice Dharma. Thereafter she did a number of solitary retreats and realized her own buddha-nature. So she sang:

> The absolute meaning is beyond comprehension by
>   the conceptual mind.
> The clarity of the natural glow (power) is unceasing.
> It is resonating, but beyond expressions of language.
> It is clear, but beyond description in words.

One day she wished to see the Fifteenth Karmapa, far away in Tsurphu, and instantly found herself before him receiving blessings. Neither the attendants of Karmapa nor her own companions were aware of her visit to Karmapa, or of her absence from her own retreat hut.

She could reach wherever she applied her concentration. She was able to speak many languages both known and unknown.

Shugseb Lochen Chönyi Zangmo was a famous Dharma propagator who filled her life with miracles.

She could pass through walls. Her body was filled with heat and her mind was filled with bliss. She could hardly stop singing or dancing. Her mind remained indivisible from its awakened nature, where there are no middle or extremes.

Then she herself had the experience of "a returner from death." One day she fell down on the ground, her body became cold, and her breathing ceased, but there was a tiny amount of warmth at her heart. During her death experience, for three whole weeks her mind, the consciousness, visited the pure land of Guru Padmasambhava, traveled through the bardo, visited the Lord of Death, and saw the sufferings of beings in various realms.

Khenpo Ngagchung was a great scholar and adept who remembered his past life.

In the latter part of her life she spent almost fifty years near Kangri Thökar, teaching many monks, nuns, and laypeople, rich and poor. She passed away at the age of eighty-nine and a number of her tulkus were recognized.

KHENPO NGAGCHUNG (1879–1941)[18]

Many miracles accompanied this teacher's birth. When he was only a year old, he and his mother were suffering from the cold of the freezing winter in the high mountains of Eastern Tibet. The boy instantly started doing heat-yoga meditation and suddenly he became so hot that his mother found it unbearable, as if she was sitting by a fire. Whereupon she asked, "Who are you, a demonic child?" To which the boy proclaimed,

I came from Labrang.
I have control over air and heat energies.
I have accomplished the trainings on Guhyasamaja.
If you could recognize me, I am Alag Rigdra.

Alag Rigdra was a famous Gelug scholar and adept of Labrang
Monastery of Amdo Province, but the boy's mother had never
heard the name Alag Rigdra before.

THE FOURTH DODRUPCHEN RINPOCHE, THUPTEN THRINLY PALZANG (1927–)[19]

This great master exhibited numerous miraculous signs both
before and after his birth. At the age of four, pointing a fin-
ger at the mountain covered by a forest called the Forest of
Many Birds from a far distance, he correctly insisted that the
hermitage of his previous life was there. He also picked up a
one-page prayer composed by his precious incarnation from
a bundle of hundreds of loose sheets. He read it loudly from
memory and gave it to his father. Now and then he would start
describing various visions or suddenly start reciting unknown
verses of profound meaning. The following lines were among
those that he recited one evening when he was not yet five, and
his attendants tried to catch them and jotted some down:

I am inseparable from the enlightened state.
I am the changeless vajra enlightenment.
I have attained the Great Bliss
Of the vajra and womb of the yogis and yoginis!

The vital-essence of the changeless vajra sphere
With the vajra protectors—to you I praise!
I am the vajra master!
I have attained the Great Bliss.

When the attending monks gave him candies and asked
questions, he would tell amazing stories, such as the details of

Guru Padmasambhava's pure land from where he returned to take rebirth.

Q: "Where do you come from?"

A: "From Zangdok Palri."

Q: "What does Zangdok Palri look like? "

A: Folding his tiny hands in the form of a mountain, he said, "It is like this."

Q: "Who lives there?"

A: "Guru Rinpoche."

Q: "Who else is there?"

A: "Avalokitesvara is there."

Q: "Do you know Raksha Thötreng, the King of the Raksas?"

A: "Yes"

Q: "What does he look like?"

A: "Many mouths, many eyes, colorful." And he laughed.

But since the age of seven, with the exception of a few important occasions, he stopped displaying any miracles or talking about his visions. He also discouraged other tulkus from showing their power.

TULKUS WHO EXHIBIT THEIR UNIQUE QUALITIES IN CHILDHOOD

Many tulkus show amazing miracles and wisdom that they have realized in their previous incarnations.

THE THIRD DODRUPCHEN RINPOCHE (1865–1926)[20]
Once, when this great teacher was a very young boy and was having a hard time learning his lessons, he had a dream in which he was blessed by the master Do Khyentse. This suddenly awakened the brilliance of the wisdom knowledge that he had realized in his past lives. At the age of seven, he gave

teachings on the *Bodhicaryavatara* to a huge assembly headed by his own teacher, the famous Patrul Rinpoche. At the age of twenty-one, he composed the first of his two most scholarly commentaries on the *Guhyagarbha Tantra*. He became one of the greatest learned masters of Nyingma history.

SERA KHANDRO DEWE DORJE (1892–1940)[21]

This great yogini was known as a tulku of Yeshe Tsogyal, the consort of Guru Rinpoche and many others. She is an exemplar, similar to many tulkus who pursued the missions of their incarnation from childhood, even when it seemed almost impossible to succeed. Throughout her childhood and teenage years, and even into adulthood, she received transmissions and prophesies in many pure visions of wisdom dakinis and adepts.

Sera Khandro Dewe Dorje was born as a beautiful princess in a rich and influential noble family in Lhasa, the capital of Tibet. While she was still in her early teens, her father arranged her future marriage. The princess strongly wished to dedicate her life fully to Dharma, and she vehemently opposed the marriage arrangement. Finally, after attempting to commit suicide, she successfully undid the arranged engagement.

One day, a group of rugged nomad pilgrims from Golok province arrived in Lhasa, after many months on the harsh trail. By chance, they camped on the compound of Sera Khandro Dewe Dorje's family palace. Through a window, the young princess looked down on the coupound and glimpsed Tulku Drime Ozer (1881–1924), the leader of the pilgrims. She instantly felt an immense devotion to the tulku, and from that point forward, he became the innate symbol of her spiritual direction.

Before long, the time came for the pilgrims to return to their home. The fourteen year old princess renounced her possessions and made a dangerous escape in order follow the pilgrims.

From that day forth, Sera Khandro Dewe Dorje's life changed drastically. She had to learn how to beg for food to survive. Her

*Sera Khandro left her privileged home at age fourteen
and became a great* ter *discoverer.*

fancy clothes gave her little protection when crossing the harsh
terrain of the high northern plateaus of Tibet. And her fancy,
flimsy shoes gave up on her. The young princess had to keep
up with the caravan by walking and running barefoot month
after month with little or sometimes no food. Because of their
ignorance and prejudice, no pilgrim would extend any support
or protection to the princess. She hardly had any opportunity
to exchange words with the tulku, as he was always strictly
guarded. But she used all of these difficult circumstances to
invigorate her spiritual dedication.

The party finally reached their home in Golok, and even there Sera Khandro Dewe Dorje endured harsh treatment from wild and jealous nomads. For over a decade she survived by taking on the lowly job of caring for the animals of nomad families. Despite these hardships, she didn't once consider returning to the luxuries of her home in Lhasa. And during this time, she continuously received transmissions and prophesies in pure visions, enjoying the highest spiritual ecstasies with total dedication to serving the dharma and the lineage of Guru Rinpoche—the sole mission of her reincarnation.

At the age of thirty, Sera Khandro Dewe Dorje became the consort of Tulku Drime Ozer. For the last few years of Tulku Drime's life, the two of them discovered many *ters* (the mystical revelations of esoteric teachings) together. Sera Khandro Dewe Dorje also wrote a number of scholarly texts and became a highly respected teacher of esoteric Dharma, with many mystic followers.

TULKUS RECOGNIZED BY HIGH LAMAS

The overwhelming number of tulkus of Tibet have been recognized by highly enlightened living lamas. About three or four years after the passing of a lama, his or her disciples could turn to a highly respected lama or lamas to seek their enlightened prophesies about where and how they would find the tulku of their deceased lama. Relying on the power of their own realization, prayers, ceremonies, and meditation, these lamas would find the tulku by means of clairvoyance, visions, dreams, or other indications.

RIGDZIN TENPE GYALTSEN, A FOURTH DODRUPCHEN (1927–61)[22]

This great teacher, also known as Riglo Rinpoche, was held in prison hundreds of miles away from his home valley, and for years no one had any information about how he was doing.

*Rigdzin Tenpe Gyaltsen
was clairvoyant and
miraculous, but he chose
to die in prison.*

Then one day, in 1961, Tulku Wangchen Nyima, the eldest
son of Apang Tertön, suddenly said, "Tulku Riglo Rinpoche
has died." Then, many months later, he said, "Tulku Riglo
Rinpoche has reincarnated in the family of Guru (or Puru)
Sodan." Years later, people found that Tulku Wangchen
Nyima's prophesies had been precisely correct regarding the
times of the passing away of Rinpoche in a prison and the
birth of a son in Guru Sodan's family.

In 1993, as the situation relaxed, the son of Guru Sodan
was recognized and enthroned as the rebirth of the Fourth
Dodrupchen Rinpoche and was named Tulku Jigme Long-
yang Rinpoche. He is fully dedicating his life to rebuilding the
Dodrupchen Monastery, returning it to its former glory, and
propagating the teachings.

Dilgo Khyentse Rinpoche (above), 1910–91, was a sublime Buddhist master and Khyentse Yangsi Rinpoche (right), b. 1993, is his incarnation.

DILGO KHYENTSE RINPOCHE (1910–91) [23]

This great master taught both deep philosophical subjects and simple stories in the same effortless fashion, like the flow of a stream. He was endowed with a steadfast memory, even in his advanced age. He was the holder of all the Buddhist lineages of Tibet, but was always searching for new ones. With a gentle smile, he ceaselessly traveled around the world sharing his wisdom light with all who are open. That was the goal and the joy of his life.

In September 1991, in his eighty-first year, while residing in Bhutan, his physical health declining, Khyentse Rinpoche persisted in giving advice and blessings to his heart disciples,

both individually and in groups. On the twenty-fourth, he formally performed for himself a self-empowerment as the final
meditation rites. On the twenty-fifth, he wrote the following
on a piece of paper and left it on the table: "On the nineteeth,
I will surely die." (The nineteenth of the Tibetan calendar
equates to September 28th of the Western calendar.) On the
twenty-eighth, in the early hours of the morning, he made an
offering to the *dharmapalas* to thank them for their past service
and to remind them to continue to serve the Dharma in the
future. Finally, later that day, the Dharma activities of his present incarnation dissolved.[24] His life was a true example of a
sublime tulku manifestation. Trulshik Rinpoche (1923–), the
chief disciple of Khyentse Rinpoche, had a vision, which he
described in this way: "I had a dream, but I wasn't asleep." In

that dreamlike vision, Khyentse Rinpoche appeared to him
and sang a poem that clearly indicated the place where he
would take rebirth and the names of his future parents. Other
lamas agreed with his vision and all recognized Tenzin Jigme
Lhundrup as the tulku of Khyentse Rinpoche.[25]

THE FOURTH DODRUPCHEN RINPOCHE (1927–)[26]

The Fifth Dzogchen Rinpoche had written down the following clear prophecy on how to find the tulku of the Third
Dodrupchen:

> The Glorious Mountain of Ngayab Subcontinent and
> The great *sambhogakaya* pure land of the Center
> Are the main sources of the manifestations of the vajra
>   master, the lord of all the buddha-lineages.
> He has four manifestations—of body, of speech, of mind,
>   and of virtues.
> The manifestation of his action
> Has taken birth in the south of the monastery,
> At a place with precious mountains, rocks, and trees,
> To a skillful means [father] and a wisdom [mother]
>   named "Ka" and "Da."
> A noble child has been born in the Earth Hare year.
> He will benefit the Dharma and beings.
> At the request of the faithful,
> This is written by the Fifth Dzogchen Tulku,
>   named Vajra.

Accordingly, at about two days' distance south from the
monastery, a search team of monks found a three-year-old
child in a village that was situated at the foot of hills covered
with rocks and trees. His father's name was Drala and mother
was Kali Kyid. Their young child had been exhibiting many
miraculous signs since his conception. The child recognized
a disciple of his previous incarnation and called him by his
name, and he gave everyone blessings by reciting OM AH HUNG

Fourth Dodrupchen Rinpoche remembered his past life and recalled being in a Buddhist pure land.

BADZAR GURU PADMA SIDDHI HUNG. Now and then he would recite a number of prayers from memory but without having learned them. When the list of possible candidates was brought back to the Fifth Dzogchen Rinpoche, he instantly picked the present Dodrupchen's name as the true tulku of the Third Dodrupchen without paying any attention to the other names. The Fourth Dodrupchen Rinpoche was enthroned at the Dodrupchen Monastery at the age of four.

For more than half a century, as prophesied by the previous masters,[27] the Dodrupchen Rinpoche has been residing in the forests of the Hidden Land[28] of Sikkim. He remains far away from the hassling activities and glamorous lifestyles desired by modern culture. Through the power of his unstinting love and enlightened wisdom, he is preserving and disseminating the authentic teachings of the vajrayana and reaching the lives of so many poor and rich people alike.

Pema Norbu Rinpoche was a key figure in rebuilding the Nyingma tradition in exile and he recognized many tulkus, including Westerners.

THE THIRD PEMA NORBU RINPOCHE (1932–2009)[29]

The Fifth Dzogchen Rinpoche also gave instructions on how to find the tulku of the Second Pema Norbu with the following prophecy:

> In the upper region of excellent Powo land,
> At the foot of majestic hills of rocks,
> Adorned with various trees and lakes,
> With a large cool river flowing from the south,
> A couple with the names of Sönam and Kyi,
> Will have a noble son of the Water Monkey year.

*The Fifth Dzogchen Rinpoche was famous for recognizing
many tulkus through his clairvoyance.*

There are great virtuous signs that he will benefit the
Dharma and beings.
I see that he will be a source of benefits to the Dharma
and beings.

The Third Pema Norbu Rinpoche became one of the greatest forces in preserving and disseminating the centuries-old
authentic tradition of intellectual scholarship, monastic discipline, and meditation accomplishments of both exoteric and
esoteric teachings of Nyingma in India and in many other
countries.

The Fourteenth Dalai Lama is the presence of
wisdom and loving-kindness.

THE FOURTEENTH DALAI LAMA (1935–)[30]

A former regent of Tibet, the Fifth Radreng, performed ceremonies at the Lhamoe Latso, a sacred lake in Central Tibet, for indications of how to find the tulku of the Thirteenth Dalai Lama. He saw three letters in the sacred lake, *a, ka,* and *ma.* He also saw the images of a monastery with jade-green and golden roofs and a house with turquoise tiles.

A year later, one of the search teams reached Amdo Province and observed the famous Kubum Monastery with its golden and jade-green roofs. Then, nearby, they also saw the village of Tagtser with its turquoise tiles. There they found a two-year-old boy. The boy saw Ketsang Rinpoche of Sera Monastery among the search group and recognized him, calling him "*Sera A-khu,*" which means "lama from Sera Monastery." When the boy was given two rosaries, two hand drums, and two walking sticks, he took the ones that had belonged to the Thirteenth Dalai Lama. That *A* letter that the Fifth Radreng saw in the sacred lake was the indication for Amdo Province. *Ka* and *Ma* were for the Karma Shartsong Hermitage situated near Tagtser village. At the age of five, the boy was officially enthroned as H. H. the Fourteenth Dalai Lama.

The Dalai Lama, a Buddha of Compassion in human form, is ceaselessly turning on the light of "good heart" in the lives of so many beings all over the globe.

TULKUS PROPHESIED IN THE DISTANT PAST

Many tulkus were prophesied by the great adepts of the past, even centuries ago. For example, Khyentse'i Wangpo, an incarnation of Jigme Lingpa, was prophesied clearly by Nyang Nyima Ozer when he wrote,

> In front of a mountain called Tsegang,
> On a boulder of the coiling of the lord of *nagas*,
> Will come a person called Lord Jampe-yang.
> He will discover thirteen profound *ters*.[31]

TULKUS WHO DISCOVER TREASURES (*TER*) THROUGH THE POWER OF THEIR PAST MEMORIES

One of the amazing sources for learning the depth and scope of the power and wisdom of the tulku system is the tradition of ter, or *terma*.[32] It is the tradition of mystical revelation of ter, the Dharma treasures of the Nyingma tradition.[33]

In the ninth century Guru Padmasambhava, the founder of Buddhism in Tibet, concealed numerous esoteric teachings and wisdom in the enlightened nature of his disciples in Tibet through his mystical power. Starting from the eleventh century, and right up to this day, thousands of tulkus of Guru Padmasambhava's direct disciples have continued to discover those concealed teachings by awakening the memories of them as well as the realizations from the enlightened nature of their minds. These memories and realizations are always vivid, as if they had been received from the guru only yesterday. Those discovered teachings are called *ter* and the discoverers are known as *tertöns*,[34] or "treasure discoverers."

There are two main categories of ters. First, thousands of tertöns have discovered "symbolic scripts"[35] written on pieces of paper as well as full texts and religious materials miraculously imprinted on the earth, on rocks, in lakes, or in the sky. In most cases, those symbolic scripts and objects turned into the keys of the real discovery, the awakening of memories of whole ranges of wisdom and teachings from the enlightened nature of their minds. Those teachings could be the length of a few words or the span of many volumes. They were entrusted to the tertöns in their previous lives by Guru Padmasambhava centuries ago. Such discoveries or discovered teachings and texts are called "earth treasures"[36] as they are discovered by relying on physical objects—the symbolic scripts or texts—as the keys.

Second, in numerous cases, tertöns discovered such wisdom and teachings solely through the power of their own wisdom-mind without relying on any physical keys. Such discovered teachings are called "mind treasures"[37] since the tertöns discovered them from their memory banks with the keys of their own wisdom-power without relying on any earthly or physical objects as the keys.

MIGYUR DORJE (1645–67)[38]

As soon as this lama, when still a very young child, started speaking, he told people that he was Thrulzhig Wangdrag

Gyatso, and spoke of the kinds of meditations he had done in his previous life. It is said that Migyur Dorje remembered two hundred of his previous lives. Without relying on studies, he became a learned master because of the power of the realizations that he had attained in his past lives. From the age of eleven, he started discovering and decoding his famous ter teachings known as *Namchö,* "the Cycle of Space Treasures,"[39] in eleven volumes. He died at the age of twenty-three with astonishing signs.

Most of the tertöns have been learned and miraculous, and they live the householder's life. They are the tulkus of highly realized disciples of Guru Padmasambhava. However, while many of them may have been recognized as tulkus in their childhood, others became known as tulkus only after they started discovering ters in their adulthood.

RECOGNITION AND ENTHRONEMENT CEREMONIES

In many cases, after finding the tulkus of high lamas, some followers and authorities from the seats of the previous lamas will go to the homes of the young tulkus to offer a simpler ceremony called "the naming ceremony."[40] In that ceremony the children will be officially named as the tulkus of the respective lamas by the senior lamas, and will be dressed in religious attire.

After a few months or so, the authorities will arrange the larger ceremonies at the monasteries or the nunneries of the deceased lamas. These are "the enthronement ceremonies."[41] First, led by a senior lama, the lamas will perform the ceremony of purification. Then they will escort the young tulku to the ceremonial throne. Then they will perform the detailed long-life empowerment with various symbolic offerings and prayers as prescribed by the traditional liturgies. At the end, the whole community will participate by receiving blessings from the tulku and making offerings of prayers and material gifts to the tulku and to his family members and relatives. Everyone will also enjoy elaborate feasts and celebrations.

During such ceremonies, people are ever-watchful of the new tulkus to see if the little ones show any special power. When the Fourth Dodrupchen Rinpoche was enthroned at the Dodrupchen Monastery at the age of four in 1931, he sat quietly on the throne for the duration of the long ceremony. But as soon as the ceremony was finished, he got up and, laughing, recited the full Seven-Line Prayer of Guru Padma-sambhava and the beginning verses of an invocation prayer of Guru Rinpoche and the *dakinis* without rehearsal.[42] Everyone present was moved and astonished.

· 7 ·

Miraculous Deaths

THERE HAVE BEEN numerous tulkus—of the buddhas, of adepts, and of meritorious lamas—in Tibet, and they have served the Dharma and beings with amazing wisdom and miraculous power. The way that masters prove that they are tulkus and that they have acquired the power to manifest tulkus in the future is by exhibiting true spiritual power. They always perform miracles while they are alive, but especially at the time of their death.

Whoever shows true spiritual miracles at the time of death will manifest tulkus with beneficial power in the future. There is no end of beings to be served, so no end of the aspirations, attainments, and actions of tulkus serving them in appropriate forms. So, just as there are great numbers of tulkus today, there will continue to be great numbers in the future.

We must remember, as we discussed earlier, that scholarship and service to others will generate great merit, which is the source of peaceful, joyful, and beneficial lives and rebirths. But the attainment of high realization in the mind-stream such as comes with full enlightenment and the high attainment of an adept can only be achieved through the power of meditation. Therefore, meditation alone will empower us to serve others in a greater way.

Miracles may be exhibited whenever they are beneficial, both during the lifetimes of the masters and at the time of their death. However, the display of power at the time of death has special significance. It is the time that a meditator reaches

the climax of his or her spiritual life. It is day one of enjoying
the ultimate fruit of one's lifelong dedication. It is the point at
which ordinary existence becomes transformed into the enlightened state. It is the time when masters show the true color
of their attainments. And because it can be such a low time for
their followers, it is the time when inspiration and consolation
are especially needed. Even so, the signs of power that ordinary
people see may not be the actual transformations or the true attainments that are taking place, because the minds of ordinary
people may be open to seeing only some limited glimpses of
such amazing qualities of great realization.

The kinds of miracles that great masters exhibit at the time
of their death can vary. Some dissolve their minds into enlightenment, the primordial state, without leaving behind any
conceptual thought. Some dissolve both their minds and their
physical bodies into primordial nature, without leaving a mortal body behind. Some, having dissolved into the primordial
nature, transform their physical body into a body of light for
service to others. Some fly away through the sky to pure lands
accompanied by lights and music. However, a greater number
of adepts leave behind *ringsel*[1] and Buddha images in their ashes
at the time of cremation. Frequently, as well, the sky may be
covered with rainbow light of various colors and designs. The
atmosphere may be filled with soothing sound. The air might
be enriched with a sweet aroma. It is therefore reasonable to
believe that if such masters possess the power to display such
miracles, they will have the power and aspirations to manifest
tulkus for the service of many.

Earth, water, fire, air, and space—the five elements—are the
building blocks of the mortal body and of all physical phenomena. They constitute the objects of mental grasping and
emotional craving for us ordinary beings. As the result of
these elements, the cycle of mental and emotional conflicts
and clashes are created and maintained, and the sensations of
pain and excitement remain active.

When meditators attain enlightenment, they attain freedom from grasping at and craving those mental and emotional objects. Soon, through the skills of specific esoteric meditations, the grasping concepts and emotional afflictions of the mind will be liberated and the five emotional afflictions will arise as the five wisdoms. At that point the five gross elements—earth, water, fire, air, and space—dissolve into their pure subtle qualities—yellow, white, red, green, and blue light. Next the wisdom and the lights will merge and become one, and this is known as the union of wisdom and wisdom-light. Buddha and Buddha pure land, emptiness and appearances, wisdom and love, wisdom and bliss, subject and object—all abide as one union, the innate union of awareness and appearances. That is buddhahood, the unborn primordial nature of all.

MIRACULOUS DEATHS OF TULKUS OF THE OLD TANTRA LINEAGE OF TIBET

There are two major lineages of tantra, or esoteric Buddhism, in Tibet. They are known as Nyingma, "the Old Tantra lineage," and Sarma, "the New Tantra lineage."[2] The Nyingma school of Tibetan Buddhism follows the old tantra lineage; all the other schools follow the New Tantra lineage. First, I will mention a few miraculous life stories of the enlightened masters from the old tantra and Dzogchen lineage as examples of the signs of their high attainments at death. This will be followed by a few miraculous life stories of the enlightened masters of the New Tantra lineages—Kadam, Kagyu, Sakya, and Gelug.

To illustrate the signs of high realization at death that the tulkus of all the lineages of Tibet manifested, I will try to detail the miraculous signs exhibited at death by the tulkus of the Old Tantra Lineage, as I am a little bit more familiar with this lineage. There are seven categories of these miraculous signs of accomplishment.

The Attainment of Rainbow Body[3]

Hundreds of Dzogchen adepts in Tibet have realized rainbow body by means of the meditation of Cutting Through.[4] They dissolve their mind into the ultimate nature (Tib., *ch'os nyid*), and the particles of their physical body into the primordial state (Tib., *rang sa*). They do this by cutting off their grasping at objects, the source of conflict and pain. The result of this is that these adepts dissolve their gross bodies gradually at the time of their death while displaying circles, beams, and auras of colorful light. Their bodies become smaller and smaller, and within a few days they totally dissolve, leaving behind only the nails and hair.

NYANG TINGDZIN ZANGPO (NINTH CENTURY)

This adept, a disciple of Vimalamitra, attained rainbow body in the cave of Trag Lhalu[5] in Lhasa. He is known as the first Tibetan master to do this.[6] Around that time, Bairotsana and his disciple, the eighty-five-year-old Pang Mipham Gonpo, also attained rainbow body. From then until this day, hundreds of meditators have attained rainbow body this way.

PADMA DUDDUL (1816–72)[7]

Born in Nyag-rong, Padma Duddul became a great teacher and adept of Dzogchen. At the age of fifty-seven, he called his disciples into the tent where he was living and gave them some final teachings and blessings. Then he told them, "Now, sew up the door of my tent and don't come back for seven days." On the morning of the seventh day, the disciples opened the tent door and were unable to find him or his body, with the exception of his hair, fingernails, and toenails, while his clothes remained on his seat. With great sadness, his disciples prayed to him. Many saw him in pure visions and received teachings and transmissions. They also felt the earth shake, while the sky was filled with lights of different colors and designs.

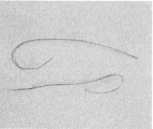

Padma Duddul attained rainbow-body and left only his hair (seen above) and nails behind.

SÖNAM NAMGYAL (1874?–1952/3)

This adept came from Yilhung Valley in Kham and was the father of the late Lama Gyurtrag, a close Dharma brother of mine and himself an accomplished meditator. What follows are the words of Lama Gyurtrag himself, just as he said them to me:

> My father was a hunter in his youth. But later he became a very devout meditator, though we didn't know how accomplished he was with his Dzogchen meditation. He was very secretive about his meditation experiences. We knew that he had completed the Fivefold Hundred-Thousand Preliminary Practices thirteen times. He had received Dzogchen meditation instruction from Jinpa Zangpo, a disciple of Do Khyentse Yeshe Dorje. He spent most of his life carving images, mantras, and scriptures on stones at Mani Kadgo in Yilhung Valley and other places.

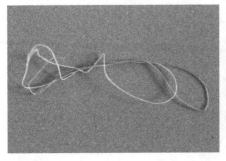 

Sönam Namgyal's mole-hair (left) and a piece of nail (right) remained behind when he dissolved into rainbow-body at the time of his death.

I was in a meditation retreat, when my brother came to see me and said, "Father is slightly sick. I don't see anything serious, but he is saying he is dying." After a couple of days, on the evening of the seventh day of the fourth month of the Water Dragon year (1952), father died at the age of seventy-nine. A local lama had advised my brother that he should take special care of his father's body, but my brother didn't understand what he really meant. So, soon after Father's death, his body was arranged as the body of an ordinary layperson. But people started noticing beams, circles, and auras of lights of different colors and sizes appearing in and around the house. Father's body kept reducing in size. Finally, they realized that father was attaining enlightenment and that his gross body was dissolving into rainbow body. After a couple of days, Father's whole body had disappeared. I concluded my retreat and rushed home. By then Father's body had already gone and only the twenty fingernails and toenails and the hair of his body were left behind at the spot where his body had been kept.

My father was extremely humble and no one ever expected him to be such a special person. If a famous lama died in this manner, it would not surprise people, but when a humble layperson displays such a great accomplishment, it amazes many. In truth, humble life is a great asset for meditation and accomplishment, but ordinary people do not see things in that light. Most people respect only hollow names, deceitful material riches, and arrogant intellectual reasoning.

The Attainment of Rainbow Body of Great Transference[8]

Highly attained adepts, through the meditations of the direct approach of Dzogchen,[9] not only dissolve their mind and body into primordial nature, but they transform them into subtle bodies of light in order to serve others. Then, they live in such a body as long as it is beneficial for others, appearing whenever and wherever they can serve.

VIMALAMITRA (VISITED TIBET IN THE NINTH CENTURY)[10]

This great master was born in India. He attained rainbow body of great transference through the Heart Essence trainings of Dzogchen.[11] He went to Tibet in the ninth century and taught Dzogchen there for years. His followers say that he still lives in Wu Tai Shan in China, and people of pure mind will see and receive teachings from him. Later Chetsun, Zangton and many others received teachings from Vimalamitra in his form as rainbow body of great transference.

PADMASAMBHAVA (VISITED TIBET IN THE NINTH CENTURY)[12]

This fully-enlightened master was born by lotus-birth[13] in India and attained rainbow body of great transference. He established Buddhism in Tibet at the beginning of the ninth century. It is believed that he manifested the Copper-Colored

Guru Padmasambhava was the founder of Tibetan Buddhism who concealed numerous esoteric teachings and objects as sacred treasures (ter).

Mountain Pure Land and still lives there. Whoever meditates on and prays to him will take rebirth in his pure land.

CHETSUN SENGE WANGCHUG (ELEVENTH CENTURY)[14]
This teacher was born in Tibet and was an exceptionally learned meditator. Vimalamitra appeared in the form of rainbow body of great transference and conferred on him Innermost Essence teachings. He meditated for seven years and attained rainbow body of great transference in the Uyug Valley.[15] Centuries later, Khyentse'i Wangpo received Chetsun Nyingthig teachings from Chetsun himself, and Vimalamitra and Chetsun are both in the rainbow body of great transference.[16]

KHADROMA KUNGA BUM[17]

This teacher was known as a tulku of Yeshe Tsogyal. She received many teachings and did strict retreats, including a seven-year retreat in Drag Yangdzong in Central Tibet. She discovered ter teachings, served many disciples, and—with a display of miracles—also discovered the sacred cave of Drag Yangdzong. At the end, her gross body dissolved into vajra rainbow light without leaving anything behind.

Flying Away to Pure Lands without Leaving a Trace

YESHE TSOGYAL (EIGHTH CENTURY)[18]

This extraordinary teacher was an incarnation of Sarasvati Buddha. She was born at Dragda in Central Tibet, and her birth was accompanied by many miraculous manifestations. Later, she became the spiritual consort of Guru Padmasambhava and traveled with him to numerous caves, forests, and mountains all over Tibet performing esoteric exercises and rites and blessing them as sacred places. Of all beings, she was the most important support for Guru Padmasambhava in transmitting and concealing as ter hundreds of thousands of teachings and religious objects in various places through their wisdom power. At the end of her life, instead of leaving her physical body behind, she flew away through the sky to Zangdok Palri, the manifested pure land of Guru Padmasambhava, and lives there.

JOMO MENMO (1248–83)[19]

This teacher was known as a tulku of Yeshe Tshogyal. When she was five, her mother died and she had to tend the domestic animals. One day, in a vision, Vajravarahi Buddha, entrusting her with a sacred text, empowered her, wherewith she enjoyed a sacred feast with the assembly of practitioners. Since that time, a stream of sacred teachings burst spontaneously from her with no need of learning. She continually danced and sang sacred dances and songs as if she were a born dancer and singer. She

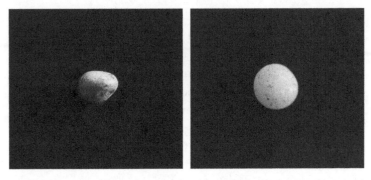

Some ringsel *(relics) emerged from the cremated bones of the highly realized Dzogchen adepts Kunkhyen Longchen Rabjam (left) and Dharma Senge (right).*

was able to see what thoughts people were having. She became the consort of the great tertön Guru Chöwang, and they helped each other to decode sacred ter teachings. Wandering in many places in South, West, and Central Tibet, she served many beings. Finally, at the age of only thirty-six, accompanied by two realized attendants, they flew up into the sky higher and higher and went toward Zangdog Palri without leaving their bodies behind. Nomadic girls and boys tending domestic animals in nearby grassy valleys saw them flying away. Children picked up and ate the remains of the feast offerings that they had left, and these caused all of them to experience a deep meditative state.

Many lamas, throughout the centuries, are known as her tulkus in Tibet.

Leaving with Miracles, Lights, and Ringsel

Numerous great masters produced great miracles of visions and displays, and many died with miraculous signs of earthquakes, musical sounds, sweet aromas, and rainbow lights in various colors and designs. Or many left in the ashes of their cremation many ringsel as the signs of high attainments and as their sacred gifts to the devotees.

JETSUN MIGYUR PALDRON (1699–1769) [20]

This great teacher is known as a tulku of both Yeshe Tsogyal and Machig Labdron. She was a daughter of Minling Terchen, the famed luminary tertön and author of important texts of the Nyingma lineage. As soon as she was born, sitting up, she sang the sacred syllable HUM.

She received extensive teachings and transmissions from her father, her uncle Lochen Dharmasri, and many others. At the age of sixteen, her father passed away. At the age of nineteen, the forces of Dzungar Mongols destroyed Mintrolling Monastery and assassinated Lochen Dharmasri along with many masters. However, Jetsun, with her mother and two sisters, escaped to Sikkim.

After the defeat of the Dzungars in Tibet, she went back and devoted her whole life to rebuilding Mintrolling and giving teachings and sacred transmissions. She also remained in retreat for many years at Khachod Dechenling. At the age of seventy-one—now even more youthful and radiant than before—sitting up in lotus posture and glancing up into the sky, she passed away. After passing, her mind and body remained in meditation for three days.

During the cremation, a ball of white smoke rose upward and moved toward the western direction. Some birds kept circling the smoke in the sky throughout the cremation ceremony. Every seventh day after her passing, for many weeks, the amazingly clear sky appeared filled with beautiful white rainbow lights. Monks and nuns of the monastery made three ceremonial visits to her sacred body. Each time five-colored rainbow light arched around the temple. Also a beam of very bright five-colored rainbow light appeared linking one mountain to another, and under that another beam of five-colored rainbow light appeared linking one major temple to another. Many colorful lights appeared in the forms of various offering objects, such as a wheel, a horse, and flowers with four petals. On her cremated bones the images of many deities and sacred syllables appeared.

Jamyang Khyentse'i Wangpo was the incarnation of many past adepts and he manifested six famous Tulkus simultaneously.

KHYENTSE'I WANGPO (1820–92)[21]

This teacher was born in Kham. From childhood he had many visions and remembered his past lives and the teachings that were practiced and taught in them. Lamas of the Nyingma lineage recognized him as the tulku of Jigme Lingpa. He remembered being Jigme Lingpa in one of his past lives and revealed an enormous amount of ter. The lamas of the Sakya tradition recognized him as the tulku of Nesar Khyentse and of Thartse Champa Namkha Chime and assigned Dzongsar, a Sakya monastery, to be his seat.

He discovered many religious objects and especially teachings through "the seven orders of transmissions":[22] the canonical tantras, earth ter, rediscovered ter, mind ter, recollected teachings, pure vision teachings, and oral teachings. These teachings were entrusted to him by Guru Padmasambhava when he was King Trisong Detsen in the ninth century. Furthermore, he received the teachings and transmissions of all the Dharma lineages that existed in Tibet and became the teacher of almost all the great students of Nyingma, Sakya, and Kagyu of his time.

One day at the age of seventy-three, he said to his attendant, "I keep seeing Amitabha Buddha in the midst of an ocean of *sangha*. I am not sure why." Another time he said, "Vimalamitra is in the sky in front of me. Can you see?" Then, early one morning, he got up, washed his hands, and said, "Now I have completed my works. Take away all the materials that are around here." Then, throwing ceremonial flowers around, he made prayers of auspiciousness for a long time. Abstaining from eating or drinking, he went into absorption until the afternoon, and then he passed away. The earth shook. His face became clear and his body became light. His disciples had various visions of him.

KHENPO KONCHOG DRONME (1859–1936)

He was born in Lushul tribe was a great scholar and an adept. He taught at the Dodrupchen monastery in Golok for many decades. The following passage in the account of Khenpo's death was written by his main disciples who were present by his side.

One evening, when he was seventy-eight years old and nursing just a minor cold while relaxing with some of his close disciples, he suddenly said,[23] "I had a dream." His disciples were sure that he had not fallen asleep. Then he continued,

A woman told me, "Sokhe Jomo[24] says, 'This present luminous absorption[25] is the realization of emptiness. Because if this is not the emptiness that is the nature of

wisdom, then the primordial Wisdom of the Ultimate
Sphere of the final buddhahood and the present luminous
absorption (at death) cannot be the same. This luminous
absorption is the king of the precious virtues.[26] Because if
all the virtues of the result are not spontaneously present
in it without (the need of) seeking (from another source),
then the wisdoms of buddhahood and the present luminous absorption will not be undifferentiable.'

I told the woman, "Yes, that is a perfect understanding.
Nevertheless, when one extends it further by meditating
on it through the (four) unmodified natural contempla-
tions[27] and when one realizes the total perfection of the
intrinsic awareness, then this (luminous absorption) becomes the five wisdoms. The clarity—without any concept that has arisen as either of the two obscurations—is
the mirrorlike wisdom. The freedom from falling into
partialities and conditions is the wisdom of evenness.
Knowing all the phenomenal existents without confusion is the distinguishing wisdom."

Then, taking a sip of soaked saffron water, he sat up in the
posture of relaxing in the natural state of mind[28] and said,
"What are you thinking!"

Instantly, Khenpo's mind merged into the luminous absorption about which he was speaking. He remained in luminous
absorption for about twelve hours or so. Then the sound of
music in the monastery aroused him from the absorption and
he passed away. During that period, as is common among
many great masters, although his pulse and heartbeat stopped,
he held up his head, his body remaining straight and maintaining a tiny heat at his heart level, which are signs that he was
still in the absorption in his body. If a meditator realizes such
luminous absorption and maintains it perfectly, then he or she
can unite with the universal luminosity, the union of awareness and emptiness. Then all the appearances spontaneously

arise as the manifestative power of the great union itself. That is the attainment of *dharmakaya,* the ultimate buddhahood.

In accordance with the tradition, after a week or so, Khenpo's body was cremated. In the ashes, they found hundreds of ringsel in white, red, yellow, and blue colors. White ringsel are common, and multiple colors are rare and are respected as a sign of the deceased having achieved full enlightenment through esoteric meditations such as Dzogchen.

KHADRO PEMA DECHEN (D. 2006)

This adept was born in Kongpo, Central Tibet. From the time of childhood she was fully inspired by Dharma and Guru Padmasambhava. At the age of sixteen, she married a great adept, Thrulzhig Pawo Dorje of Minyag, Kham. Most of the time with her husband and sometimes alone, she spent years in solitude in caves and mountains observing strict meditative practices and taking in very little food. Her retreats included shelters of rocks, clothing of rags, and quenching of thirst by hard to get water on the tops of high mountains. One time, a line of mice kept bringing tiny pieces of food and piling them up in front of her to sustain her in a cave in a high mountain. In addition to many other serious practices, she accumulated thirteen sets of the Fivefold Hundred-thousand Ngondro practice. She attained high realization, along with many visions and revelations, but kept them all secret. After the death of her first husband, she married the Fourth Dodrupchen Rinpoche and supported Rinpoche's Dharma activities so that they will flourish.

At the time of her passing, she remained in meditation for days. During her cremation, the sky was filled with rainbow lights. These were not just beams of rainbow lights, which are not that rare, but *thigles,* circles or spheres of rainbow light of multiple colors, sizes, and designs. They are signs that every particle of the physical form is being transformed into pure light, and then it all is being absorbed into the Ultimate Pure

Sphere. In fact, all that witnesses ever see is some sideshow of them. And this was witnessed by hundreds of people—Tibetans, Bhutanese, Nepalese, Chinese, and Westerners alike—and it was all documented in still photos and videos. One Westerner remarked, "I never understood why Tibetans make a big deal about rainbow lights. But seeing this, I know what it can be. It is something very special." Also in Khandro's ashes they found many ringsel. However, because the heat of the cremation fire was so strong, when they were touched, they dissolved.

Taking Rebirth in Pure Lands

CHOGYUR DECHEN LINGPA (1829–70)[29]

This great adept was a tulku of Prince Murum Tsenpo, a disciple of Guru Padmasambhava, and one of the greatest tertöns in recent centuries. He was born in Nangchen Province in Kham. He revealed thirty-nine volumes of teachings of "seven different orders of transmissions":[30] the canonical tantras, earth ter, rediscovered ter, mind ter, recollected teachings, pure vision teachings, and oral teachings. At the age of forty-two he passed away with lights and earth waves. Great master Khyentse'i Wangpo saw Chogyur Lingpa in a vision as having been born in the Lotus-Covered Pure Land[31] as a bodhisattva named Fruit of the Lotus[32] and he received transmissions.

KHENPO TSEWANG RIGDZIN (1883–1958)[33]

This teacher was born in Mewa tribal group in Amdo and became a great Dzogchen adept and teacher. A very tall and heavy man, he was unable to walk and, at the age of seventy-six, was spending time in the county prison. One day the prison guards tied him up tightly with ropes to the back of a yak and took him to the site of a public gathering, where he was to be criticized in order to "reeducate" him. On the way, when he and his police escorts reached the top of a hill, Khenpo started to

*Khenpo Tsewang Rigdzin flew away into the sky and
disappeared in front of many people.*

loudly recite the mantra of Guru Padmasambhava. At the very
moment that his guards ordered, "Don't make noise!" a strong
storm hit. This forced everyone to close their eyes briefly, and
when they opened them, Khenpo wasn't on the yak. However,
they did see that some pieces of colorful clouds were floating
over them. Suddenly they saw Khenpo, in his monk's robes,
flying up into the sky as if the clouds had picked him up and he
was being carried away. He soon disappeared into the clouds
and was never seen or heard from again.

Some say he attained rainbow body, as there were lots of colorful clouds and he disappeared without any physical remainder. Others think that he could have flown away to the pure land of Guru Rinpoche the way Yeshe Tsogyal and many adepts did, since he was praying to Guru Rinpoche at the moment that they saw him flying away.

Leaving Profound Testaments

Just as the great Dzogchen masters of India—Garab Dorje, Jampal Shenyen, and others—did, so many later great masters also transmitted their testaments or last words in pure visions[34] to their main disciples at the time of their passing away.

THE FIRST DODRUPCHEN (1745–1821)[35]

On the very night of this great adept's death, his final spiritual words were received by his principal disciple, Do Khyentse, who was at a distance of many days' travel by horse. In the latter part of the night, Do Khyentse saw Dodrupchen in a pure vision appearing in the sky in a radiant light-body and in the attire of rainbow light. He was floating on a carpet of light, which was held up by four dakinis. In a very enchanting voice and melody, Dodrupchen sang the verses of his final words:

> I am going into the expanse of the Wisdom of the
>   Ultimate Sphere,
> Which is the state that transcends thoughts and
>   expressions.
> I am going into the state of mirrorlike wisdom,
> Which is the ceaseless clear glow, fresh and open.
> I am going into the expanse of the Wisdom of Evenness,
> In which all the thoughts of grasping and grasper have
>   vanished into the Ultimate Sphere.
> I am going into the Wisdom of Distinguishing
>   Awareness,

Which is the clarity—the dawn of six kinds of
  foreknowledge.
I am going into the state of the Wisdom of
  Accomplishment,
Which emanates various manifestations in accordance
  (with the needs of) trainable beings.
I am going to Zangdok Palri, the pure land of the
  knowledge-holders.
As my mind unites as the mind of the Heruka,
I will manifest three tulkus as your companions. . . .
Be aware of samsara and nirvana as dreams and illusions.
Dedicate yourself to the meditation in which there is no
  reference point.
This is the empowerment of total entrustment and
  aspiration.
This is the supreme empowerment of the empowerments.

Beams of rainbow light of five colors emanated from the white *Ah* letter at Dodrupchen's heart and merged into Do Khyentse. Then from the *Ah* letter a second *Ah* letter emerged and merged into the heart of Do Khyentse. For a while, Do Khyentse lost his ordinary consciousness and merged into the experience of vajra waves. When he regained consciousness, Dodrupchen had disappeared. For three days, Do Khyentse remained in a state in which all thoughts had dissolved. The innate awareness had spontaneously awakened clearly in him. After a while, he felt great sadness, realizing that his lama had passed away.

Many accomplished disciples of enlightened masters receive teachings and transmissions from their teachers in pure visions while they are alive, and especially at the time of their death or later, but the main disciple may receive "the testament" at the time of the teacher's death, which makes the recipient the main lineage holder, and those words the sacred instructions.

MIRACULOUS DEATHS OF TULKUS OF THE
NEW TANTRA LINEAGE

There have been numerous masters who have displayed amazing wisdom and power at the time of their passing away in the Kadam, Kagyu, Sakya, and Gelug schools of the New Tantra lineage of Tibetan Buddhism. However, I am just picking only a few drops from the ocean of miraculous stories of tulkus from the New Tantra lineage, as my knowledge, resources, and the space in this book are limited.

Transforming the Body into Vajra Light

DRUPCHEN CHÖKYI DORJE (SEVENTEENTH CENTURY)[36]

This great teacher was a tulku of Avadhuti, a great adept in India, and the tulku of Chögyal Phagpa of Sakya. Vajrayogini appeared in a pure vision to Panchen Chökyi Gyatshen and prophesied that Chökyi Dorje would become the holder of "oral esoteric teachings"[37] of Tsongkhapa. So Panchen took care of him from the age of eleven and taught him. He meditated on "development stage" and especially on "perfection stage" of tantra at a sacred place called Pemachen at Jomo Lhari, and attained "impure illusory-body."[38] Then, in a pure vision, he received the complete "oral esoteric teachings" of Tsongkhapa—which Tsongkhapa had received from Manjusri Buddha—from Tsongkhapa himself. Then he meditated more on the perfection stage and realized the union, the vajradharahood. He remained with the body of union, the wisdom of emptiness and skillful means. But without abandoning his gross body created by karmic maturation, he kept giving teachings to many.

He waited for the right recipient of the oral esoteric teachings and continued living until he was over one hundred years

old. Finally, he found a novice of seventeen years of age, whom
he trained in Dharma. Then he taught and entrusted the complete oral esoteric teachings of Tsongkhapa only to the novice
and two other undisclosed disciples. The novice became the
famous Gyalwa Wensapa. Finally, seeing no reason for maintaining the gross body any longer, he dissolved it and remained
in vajra light-body.[39] Since then he has kept serving many
through various appearances of the vajra light-body, according
to people's receptivity. There were many stories of seeing him
and receiving teachings from him for a long time.

Going to the Pure Lands without Leaving a Body

LOCHEN RINCHEN ZANGPO (958–1055)[40]
This great teacher was born in Ngari Province in Tibet. He
visited Kashmir several times to study Sanskrit and Buddhism.
He is known as one of the greatest scholars and translators of
Tibetan Buddhist history. At the age of eighty-five, he received
additional teachings from Atisa and went into total seclusion
doing meditations. At the age of ninety-eight, filling the sky
with images of deities and with music, he left for a dakini pure
land without leaving any physical remains behind.

Displaying Great Miracles of Visions, Sounds, and Lights

JETSUN MILAREPA (1052–1135)[41]
Milarepa is one of the greatest adepts ever known in Tibet. At
the age of eighty-four, he returned to the hermitage at Chuwar, saying that is where he wanted to die. For a number of
days, people started to witness greater miracles from him than
before. A number of Milarepas appeared at many places simultaneously, performing different activities. The atmosphere
was filled with colorful rainbow lights of different designs
and musical sounds. His disciples knew that he was dying and

Milarepa was a renowned ascetic, adept, and poet.

lamented, "If you leave for a pure land, how can we pray to you?" He told his devotees, "You can pray to me as you like. I will remain with those who pray to me with devotion. I will fulfill your wishes if you pray to me from your heart. For a while I will go to see Aksobhya Buddha in the Totally Joyful Pure Land."[42] Some yogis asked, "If it helps to serve others, can we have some prosperous livelihood?" Milarepa answered, "Yes, if you have no self-cherishing thoughts; but that is very hard! If you are cherishing the desires for this life, then forget about the idea of serving others, as you are not able to achieve even your own goals. It will be like claiming to save others while you are weak and are being carried away down a stream. Until you have realized the true nature, don't rush to serve others, like the blind leading the blind. As space has no limits, so beings have no limit. If you meditate, then the opportunities for serving others will come. All of you must develop the thought of cherishing others more than yourselves. Make aspirations for attaining buddhahood for the sake of all beings." Then he sang,

> If you maintain humility, you will attain the highest goal.
> If you travel slowly, you will reach your destination fast.
> If you let go the mundane activities, you will achieve the
>   greatest goals.
> If you follow the sacred paths, you will enjoy the
>   short cuts.
> If you realize emptiness, compassion will arise in you.
> If you have compassion, there will be no distinctions of
>   self and others.
> If there are no distinctions of self and others, you will be
>   able to serve others.
> If you serve beings, you will meet me.
> If you meet me, you attain buddhahood.
> Pray to me, the buddhas and the disciples
> As if they are one.

Finally, saying the words "If you wish to listen to me, then follow me," he went into meditative absorption and passed away.

For days, the sky and earth around Chuwar kept being filled with colorful rainbow lights, divine visions, sweet aromas, and soothing music. However, his body would not catch fire until his chief disciple, Rechungpa, arrived. Some of his students received sacred transmissions from Milarepa in pure visions and many were immersed in meditative experience.

GAMPOPA (1079–1153)[43]

This great teacher was the chief disciple of Milarepa and was a physician. When his wife died, he renounced his household life and became a strictly disciplined monk and meditator. There was in him no more attachment to material things or worldly activities. He studied the teaching of the Gradual Path to Enlightenment[44] of the Kadampa tradition from Geshe Nyugrumpa, Chagripa, and others, and he studied Mahamudra and the Six Dharmas of Naropa from Milarepa. He trained himself and others by uniting both of these teaching traditions together.

At the age of seventy-five, he didn't have any sickness, but seemed weak. When a disciple asked, "How is your health?" he just sat up straight and, gazing directly into the sky, said, "Do you understand: 'In the thoughts, there is nothing but vividness?' I do!" With that he passed away. That night the sky remained filled with colorful rainbow lights. In the sky in front of Gampo Monastery, everyone witnessed 108 stupas, so beautiful and shining with rays of light, as if they were made of crystal. People also heard the sounds of a big drum being beaten. Different people experienced different visions, lights of various designs, and clouds of dakinis.

SACHEN KUNGA NYINGPO (1092–1158)[45]

Known as a manifestation of Avalokitesvara, this great adept was the son of Khon Könchok Gyalpo, the Founder of the Sakya school. Mahasiddha Virupa of India visited him miraculously to entrust to him the unique esoteric teachings of "the path and fruits."[46] He exhibited six different appearances of himself at the same time. After death, he had four manifestations in four different pure lands and places. During the cremation, disciples had different visions of him.

SAKYA PANDITA (1182–1251)[47]

This renowned teacher was known as an emanation of Manjusri Buddha, and spoke Sanskrit after his birth. He received transmissions from many masters and from many deities in pure visions. He is known as one of the greatest minds of Tibet, and wrote many scholarly treatises on logic, Dharma, and other subjects. If he studied any subject once, he learned it and would not forget. He visited Lunzhou City in China and taught Dharma to Ogedei (Gotan) Khan, the grandson of Genghis Khan. He died there at the age of seventy, accompanied by miracles. During the cremation, lights, divine images, and sweet smells filled the atmosphere, and musical sounds were heard miraculously. Images of many deities appeared in the ashes.[48]

JE TSONGKHAPA (1357–1419)[49]

Je Tsongkhapa was the founder of the Gelug school and was born in Amdo, Eastern Tibet. He is believed to have taken birth as a boy in India and developed bodhicitta in front of the Buddha. Since then he had been training in Dharma for many lives. At the place where he was born grew a tree. Each of its 100,000 leaves bore a buddha image. Later a monastery was built at that spot and was named Kubum, the Monastery of 100,000 Images.[50]

He became one of the greatest scholars of Tibetan history, produced many brilliant students, wrote eighteen volumes of monumental treatises, and built Gaden Monastery.

At the age of sixty-three, he gave his ceremonial hat and robe to Darma Rinchen, making him his successor. Throughout the night, he repeatedly performed liturgies with self-empowerments, then he remained in meditative absorption. Early the next morning, sitting in lotus posture with hands in contemplative gesture, he passed away. His face became youthful and glowed with light. The sky was filled with nets of rainbow light. He has been prophesied to take rebirth in Tusita Heaven and to become a buddha known as The Lion's Roar[51] in the future. Khedrup Je, one of his two chief disciples, saw him in five different forms in five different pure visions.

PANCHEN LOBZANG CHÖGYAN (1570–1662)

This great teacher was the First Panchen Lama;[52] however, some count him as the Fourth Panchen Lama by listing him after Khedrup Geleg Palzang, Chogkyi Langpo, and Wentsawa Lobzang Thondrup. He was the preceptor of a great many Gelug masters and the author of many important liturgical texts. He is known as the tulku of Khedrup Geleg Palzang, one of the two chief disciples of Tsongkhapa. At the age of ninety-five, saying, "Tusita Heaven is more joyful than here," he sat in meditation posture, recited some prayers, merged into luminous nature, and passed away. He remained in meditative absorption for a few days, and during that time, even though snow kept falling, rainbow tents continually arched overhead, rainbow lights shone in different designs, and never-before-heard sounds played on and off.

CHÖGYAM TRUNGPA RINPOCHE (1939–87)[53]

When the Sixteenth Karmapa was fourteen years old, he dedicated his visions to recognizing the incarnation of the Tenth Trungpa Rinpoche. They said that the Tulku of Trungpa had incarnated in a village with a name that was the composite of *ge* and *de*—that was a five-day's journey from Zurmang monastery. The door of the tulku's dwelling was facing south with a big red dog. The tulku's father's name was Yeshe Dargye. His mother's name was composed of a *chung* and *tsho*. Later the search party found the one-year-old Trungpa Tulku exactly as prophesized by the Karmapa.

Trungpa Rinpoche was born and trained in the Kham region of Tibet and was an exceptionally gifted student and accomplished master. He escaped to India as a refugee in 1959, moved to England in 1963, and finally settled in North America in 1970. He wrote amazing books in English and revealed a number of teachings. He played a pioneering role in bringing Tibetan Buddhism to the West and establishing it there. At the age of forty-nine he passed away in Halifax, Canada. During

*Chögyam Trungpa Rinpoche was one of the pioneering Buddhist
masters who established Tibetan Buddhism in the West.*

the cremation ceremony in Karmê Chöling, in Vermont, a
number of rainbow lights appeared and a rainbow completely
encircled the sun. A unique train of clouds filled the sky, making the sky turquoise and pink.

Materializing Sacred Symbols

THE FIRST KARMAPA, DÜSUM KHYENPA (1110–93)[54]
This great lama was the founder of the Karma Kagyu school and
a disciple of Gampopa. He was a tulku of Prajnanga, who was
a disciple of Nagarjuna, and of Gyalwa Chog-yang, who was a
disciple of Guru Padmasambhava. He showed his high spiritual
accomplishments throughout his life, starting in childhood. He

meditated and taught both in Central Tibet and in Kham, and established Tsurphu Monastery. One day, giving teachings on the ultimate nature, he sat up, gazed into the sky, and remained absorbed in meditation. Soon he passed away. People saw various visions, and images of seed syllables, or sacred letters, were found in his ashes.

TSANGPA GYARE YESHE DORJE (1161–1211)[55]

This great lama was known as a manifestation of Naropa. After meditating only seven days, his realization became equal to that of his teacher, Ling-repa. He was able to travel through walls without hindrance. When he was laying the foundation of his main monastery, everyone heard the roaring sounds of thunder a number of times. The word for "thunder" or "dragon" in Tibetan is *drug,* so he named the monastery Drug Gon. In addition, his teaching lineage became known as Drugpa Kagyu and his tulku lineage is known as the Drugchen Rinpoches, among whom was the luminary Pema Karpo. The present Drugchen Rinpoche is the twelfth tulku. During the cremation of his body, a tent of rainbow light arched around it, and flowers were seen to shower down. On the twenty-one vertebrae, there appeared twenty-one Avalokitesvara images.

NGORCHEN KUNGA ZANGPO (1382–1457)[56]

This great teacher was the founder of the Ngor lineage of the Sakya school and the founder of Ngor Monastery, and was prophesied in the *Lotus Sutra* by the Buddha. He received transmissions from many living masters as well as in pure visions. He became a great scholar of the whole Dharma, and especially of tantra, and became known as the Vajradhara. During his cremation, the sky was filled with light and left many ringsel in white, yellow, and other colors in the ashes.

GO RABJAMPA SÖNAM SENGE (1429–89)[57]

One of the greatest scholars of Sakya school, this great lama was known as the Omniscient One. He established Tanag Monastery in Tsang, taught at the Ngor Monastery, and authored many scholastic treatises. At the time of his death, he focused his mind to take rebirth in Amitabha's pure land by making aspirations. During the cremation, the smoke turned into designs of auspicious signs. Musical sounds were heard. The sky was filled with nets of light, and many ringsel were produced from the ashes.

Miraculous Lives

DRIGUNG KYOBPA (1110–70)[58]

This great adept was the founder of the Drigung Kagyu, and was known as a tulku of Nagarjuna and a disciple of Phagmotrupa. He healed his own leprosy through the meditation on compassion. He became so famous that fifty-five thousand disciples assembled to hear his teachings. At the time of his death, his disciples asked, "Where will you be going?" He answered, "I am not going anywhere. I will remain in the mind-streams of my disciples."

TAGLUNG THANGPA (1142–1210)[59]

The founder of the Taglung Kagyu, this great teacher was another disciple of Phagmotrupa. He was a highly learned master and lived with strict monastic discipline. Disciples kept seeing him in different forms and being in numerous places at the same time. At the time of his passing away, he said, "I have never been separated from the Buddha. We have the same mind-stream." Then he added, "If you do not get it—I am the Buddha."

Taking Rebirth in the Pure Lands

DROMTONPA (982–1055)[60]

This great teacher was known as a tulku of Avalokitesvara Buddha. He built Radreng Monastery, the seat of the Kadam school. As Tara prophesied to Atisa, Dromtonpa became his main disciple. He made the Kadam teachings the cornerstone of Buddhism in Tibet. He was a strict ascetic, but remained as a lay devotee (Skt., *upasika*). On his tongue, his teacher and others saw a small flower with Atisa on it. Some also saw him as an *Ah* syllable. At the time of his passing away, he said to his students, "You don't have to rely on a teacher alone. Read the sutras. Make the sutras your teacher. Have good thoughts and you will encounter the goodness of people." A student asked, "Are you calling bodhicitta a good thought?" He said, "Yes, it is." He took rebirth in Tusita Heaven and manifested many tulkus.

TULKUS WHO LIVE AND DIE AS ORDINARY PEOPLE

There have been, and continue to be, numerous tulkus who were highly accomplished but lived and died without showing any sign of power. Since they lived and passed away as ordinary people, hardly anyone noticed them and there are no records of their deeds or power. Such tulkus train and realize spiritual attainments quietly so that they will not fall into the trap of the rush for fame and gain. They serve others at their natural and daily-life level and produce long-lasting benefits. Through such processes, they can effectively reach those beings who are not open to structured traditions.

· 8 ·

Miracles of Adepts versus
Paranormal Events

MANY PEOPLE THINK that the miraculous lives of enlightened beings fall into the category of ordinary paranormal
events, since they tend to have no accurate or personal experience with either.

As mentioned earlier, highly accomplished adepts realize
the enlightened nature and qualities, and they thereby attain
enlightened wisdom, love, and power. They dedicate their enlightened power to serving others through appropriate manifestations. At the time of death, they can dissolve their bodies
into light, fly away to Buddha pure lands, or become fully
enlightened. All the miraculous activities that they manifest
come from the power of their own enlightened minds, and not
from external sources or the effects of negative causation.

Ordinary beings, on the other hand, may enjoy the gift of
some paranormal powers, manifested either positively or nega-
tively, and some are connected with the spirit worlds. They
may have the ability to create the illusion of appearing and
disappearing at will. They may be able to take rebirth in invisible worlds and communicate with the living. They sometimes
have the power of helping friends or hurting foes. However,
their power is fundamentally either limited or not pure; or else
it comes from others, such as from the spirit world.

The spirit world is a world system that remains invisible to
human beings unless they have karmic connection with one or

more spirits. However, if you establish any positive or negative relationships with them, you could be affected accordingly, and you could even take rebirth in such worlds of phenomena. Most of the spirit world is part of the demigods realm,[1] which is one the six realms[2] of the universe according to Buddhism. Many of the beings of the spirit worlds are present in various places on earth—mountains, rocks, lakes, rivers, and forests— as land deities.[3]

Throughout Tibetan history, as in other societies, one frequently finds people or spirits who possess paranormal powers. Such people or spirits belong to either of two categories. First, among both human beings and spirit beings, there are many who enjoy spiritual, healing, and paranormal powers that benefit themselves or others. Their power may be limited or not totally pure because it is not enlightened power. But there are also tulkus of buddhas, adepts, or virtuous beings who have enlightened power, and some of them are known as the Dharma guardians[4] in Mahayana Buddhism.

Second, among both human beings and spirit beings there are many who possess paranormal power that is harmful to themselves and others. They have accumulated some positive karmas or merits in their past, and thus have gained some power, but then have dedicated those merits for wrong purposes, such as the worldly power of controlling others for selfish purposes or hurting or eliminating those with whom they don't see eye to eye. Whatever merits they earned, they have turned them into harmful power through the emotional energies of hatred, greed, and confusion, and then they activate them. The force of such actions will cause only disharmony, pain, and confusion in the hearts of individuals and society.

Until the middle of the last century, in the wild high plateau of Eastern Tibet, chieftains would take care of their scattered pockets of tribal encampments along with taking the responsibility for defending them. Many of these chieftains worshipped spirits—the land deities of the mountains, lakes, and rivers—

and they did so for the purpose of becoming prosperous and gaining some paranormal power to defeat and destroy their foes. Many of the spirits were the rebirths of the deceased ancestors of the chieftains themselves. In addition, most of the chieftains were devout Buddhists—however, prayers to and blessings from the buddhas cause only success, peace, and enlightenment, not pain and defeat for anyone, including one's so-called foes. So by continuing to rely on the support of spirit beings, many chieftains couldn't help but take rebirth in the spirit world at the time of their death since the spirits were waiting to welcome them to their world or even to snatch their consciousnesses if necessary.[5] And although many beings in the spirit world enjoy a high degree of power and prosperity, most suffer from pain, confusion, greed, jealousy, and fighting, and have a bleak future.

In order to illustrate some paranormal events related to the spirit world, I would like to present two life stories of my own forefathers.

First, there once was a warrior[6] chieftain named Wangrol Godrug,[7] a number of generations back in my maternal lineage. One day, he went to offer a *sang*[8] at a sacred mountain and didn't return. After a couple of days, children went to look for him and found that his little tent was empty and his horse was still tied to a peg. Outside, they saw the tracks of seven steps in the snow walking toward the mountain. There they found his clothes, but not him, his body, or any more tracks. Since then his spirit is known to have communicated a number of times with people through mediums.

The second story is about my maternal grandfather, Chief Dragtsal Gonpo. He was very religious, kind, and fair with everybody. But a few weeks before his death, a neighborhood tribal group attacked his small tribal group over a bride, robbing a number of families and injuring some people. So he died with great humiliation and anger. After a number of years he started to communicate with his tribal subjects through a medium. He said, "When I died, I was ready to go to the pure land of Tara (as he was a lifelong devotee of Tara). Pushul Lama (who was his teacher and performed the funeral ceremony) gave me the directions. But my mind was suddenly distracted by the sufferings inflicted upon my poor people. At that moment, the ancestor spirits, who were waiting, caught me. I found myself trapped in the spirit world. For the first long three years, I didn't surrender to the spirit beings, as how they lived wasn't wholesome or inspiring. They kept me in chains and I sustained myself by eating pebbles. Finally, I gave up and now I am a leader with hundreds of thousands of followers." I myself can't remember him, as he died when I was three or four, but people who knew him well say that through the medium he spoke as when he was alive. He remembered the tribal secrets that only a few knew. I remember him asking me, "Boy, do you have anything to say?" I was so shy and scared, I didn't utter a word.

There was also another phenomenon in the nomadic world of Eastern Tibet, where people, especially young ones, would disappear and, in most cases, come back with strange stories. Most of them are known as having been kidnapped by *menmo*,[9] a class of spirits.

When the daughter of a friend of mine was around seven years old, she went to look after some domestic animals on the slope of a nearby mountain and suddenly disappeared. After unsuccessfully searching for three days, they invited a lama for help. Ringing a ritual bell, the lama performed a ceremony of "ransom offerings,"[10] which are offerings of food to the spirits along with prayers to the buddhas. Then that very evening, they found the girl near a rock on the mountain where they thought she had disappeared, but had been unable to see her till then.

The girl described her experiences this way: "I went to that mountain to look after some domestic animals, but it started to rain. So I quickly rushed to the rock that was overhanging to take shelter. Then I think I fell asleep. As in a dream, an old woman came and took me into her dwelling, which was filled with filthy things. I stayed there for a while. She offered me something to eat, but it looked so filthy I didn't take it. Then suddenly I started to hear the sound of a ringing ritual bell. (Under normal circumstances, the ringing sound of a bell would not reach that distance.) The woman told me, 'Now you have to go back home.' At that moment, I just felt as if I woke up. I found myself near the rock, where I remember taking shelter at the beginning. I don't have any sense of how long I slept." Among the communities of the high mountain valleys, there have long been stories of similar experiences taking place now and then.

Furthermore, there were many ordinary people who enjoyed paranormal gifts, such as predicting the future, reading others' minds, or showing magical displays, but not the power of any high spiritual realization. Some also exhibit such gifts through the supporting hands of beings of the spirit world. Some of these gifts were beneficial to others and their predictions were accurate, but some were not.

In the eleventh century, there was a herdsman called Kargyal in Ngari Province.[11] He was possessed by a *naga*[12] with wrong views. Soon, Kargyal was able to appear as a buddha and give impressive, but wrong, teachings by magically sitting in the sky. Soon he became known as Buddha Kargyal and attracted a great number of followers. The great translator and master Rinchen Zangpo knew what was going on. When Rinchen Zangpo, in meditative state, approached Kargyal, Kargyal fell on the ground and became a humble man.

According to Buddhism, it is possible for anything to appear and happen, as in a dream, if the causes and conditions are gathered and active, as everything is contrived by causes and conditions. The nature of all, similar to a stage, is totally open—like space. Every happening can manifest when the causes and conditions are active. According to karmic law,

· 9 ·

Common Questions

1. Are the tulkus recognized by well-known institutions more authentic?

Generally, the tulkus recognized by and educated in greater monasteries enjoy a greater potential for authenticity, scholarship, and accomplishments because of the availability of a stricter structure and well-organized facilities to recognize and train them. However, some simpler but well-disciplined institutions could be preserving the authenticity of Dharma and the tulku tradition more purely, as they are less exposed to the influence of external enterprises. Therefore, the best way to gauge individual tulkus' authenticity is to look at how they were recognized and especially their individual qualities and activities.

2. Is it true that most tulkus will take rebirth in the communities of their past lives?

Tulkus mostly take rebirth in the same vicinity and community where they lived their previous lives in order to continue uninterrupted the service they started and to serve the followers who were praying for their return. However, there are also many cases in which they take rebirth far from their previous locations.

3. Why do some tulkus take rebirth in prosperous families and others do not?

Tulkus may take rebirth in families that are either poor or prosperous, as each has its own purposes and merits. Taking rebirth in powerful or virtuous families could enable the tulkus to be more effective in serving their goals. Taking rebirth in poor and weak families will help the tulkus to be in touch with the real lives of grassroots people and to lift up the spirits of the families who are left out in the cold.

The Fourth Dalai Lama was born to a ruler in Mongolia in 1589. The Third Dodrupchen Rinpoche was born as one of the eight famous sons of Dudjom Lingpa, a great tertön. By contrast, Jigme Lingpa was born into a simple yogi's family, and the Thirteenth Dalai Lama was born to simple peasant parents.

4. Why do many tulkus take rebirth in virtuous families, whereas others do not?

The tulkus of buddhas or adepts might take rebirth in unvirtuous families or societies in order to improve the lives of such people through their enlightened wisdom and power.

JIGME GYALWE NYUGU (1765–1843)[1]
This master taught *The Words of My Perfect Teacher.* One day he heard of a couple who had slaughtered many sheep for a wedding, and when he died, he expressed the wish to take rebirth as the couple's son to save them from the hellish future that awaited them. Soon he was born as their child, Pema Kunzang, who became one of the kindest of teachers.

However, most tulkus of virtuous lamas take rebirth in families and societies that are devout or at least open to Dharma, so that they can get the favorable support necessary to continue their spiritual trainings and service for others.

5. Why do some tulkus display miracles at first, but later cease to do so?

Some tulkus exhibit miraculous qualities in childhood, but they lessen the frequency of such displays, or even stop them altogether, as they grow older. Others may not exhibit any power during their childhood, but start displaying miracles as they grow up, for various reasons. Many may never display any miraculous power, but are devout in Dharma, kind to all, learned in various fields, and humble in nature—the true miraculous qualities.

THE FOURTH DODRUPCHEN RINPOCHE (1927–)[2]

This great teacher exhibited numerous miracles and showed clairvoyance during his childhood. But as he grew up, he spoke against such displays and even advised others against exhibiting such power. He also clearly foresaw what political problems Tibetans were about to face and quietly escaped to India years in advance. I myself escaped with my life to India with Rinpoche, and am still breathing after more than a half century, solely because of his clairvoyance and kindness. However, when we left, Rinpoche kept what he knew mostly to himself, since he knew people wouldn't believe it until it was too late.

RIGDZIN TENPE GYALTSEN (1927–61)[3]

This great lama, on the other hand, was not known for exhibiting any special power in childhood. But ever since he was in his early teens, all of his disciples, which includes me, witnessed countless displays of miracles. He made objects move merely by looking at them, made imprints in rocks as if they were made of mud, and changed food that was enough for only three hundred monks into a feast for over a thousand. He also discovered many ter, the mystical teachings, and taught deep philosophical texts that he had not studied. For hours he would describe visions of pure lands and happenings that he was seeing. He also kept bluntly warning people that Tibetans would soon be enduring great sufferings and that time was running out for them to escape. However, he himself always kept busy giving teachings, saying prayers, doing meditations, leading ceremonies, and never wished to escape—he died in prison. Tulkus have their own roles to play and goals to fulfill.

6. Does the success of tulkus depend on the support of others?

If tulkus are offered good opportunities by their monasteries, nunneries, or communities to resume their trainings and retain their spiritual inheritances, it will be much easier for them to achieve their goals than it would be for ordinary new trainees, for they have the spiritual accumulations and experiences of many past lives to bank on. With just a little support and training, they can easily reopen the treasures of knowledge and attainment that they had been earning, storing, and maintaining in their memory reservoir for the course of many previous lives.

7. Are there tulkus who are the manifestations of multiple adepts who lived during the same period and are there many adepts who manifested many tulkus simultaneously?

Some lamas could be the tulkus of many adepts and some adepts could manifest many tulkus simultaneously. Jigme Lingpa is known as the tulku of two enlightened masters: Vimalamitra and King Trisong Detsen. Khyentse'i Wangpo manifested six recognized tulkus[4] simultaneously.

8. What do I have to do to have a tulku as my teacher?

Whether you are seriously looking for a tulku as a teacher or just searching for a teacher to learn and receive Dharma benefits, you must go through certain steps. First, look for qualified Dharma teachers. You must examine them thoroughly and repeatedly, whether they actually embody the true qualities for being a real Dharma teacher from your point of view or insofar as they live up to the following criteria: Are their minds filled with the love and rejoicing that character-ize true Dharma teachers, instead of consumed by anger and jealousy? Are they filled with knowledge and humility, instead of ignorance and arrogance? Are they filled with the gener-osity and contentment, instead of greed and discontent? Then that might be a great indication that you must look for other teachers.

After finding such a qualified teacher, you must accept him or her as your Dharma teacher. Open your heart to the person with total respect and trust. Receive the teachings that you need with total appreciation. Trust in both the teacher and the teachings with no doubts or hesitations. You will not make progress and move forward if you don't have full trust in the teachers or the teachings. You must see the teachers as enlight-ened manifestations and receive the teachings and transmis-sions as pure nectar, the true Buddhism. Then by the power of trust and the purity of the teachings, you will obtain all possible benefits from the teachers as if they were true enlight-ened manifestations, or tulkus, whether or not they have been recognized as such. So, finding an excellent teacher by careful search is the most important first step. Sakya Pandita writes,

> All the achievements of the goals—from now
> Up to the attainment of buddhahood—
> Depend on the excellent teachers.
> But people are accepting whoever is available
> Without examining and analyzing them,
> Like picking up goods in a cheap fair.
> Alas! People of the dark age are strange.[5]

There are ten qualities that Dharma teachers must enjoy. Asanga lists them:

You should have a teacher who is tamed (with moral disciplines), peaceful (with contemplation), very

peaceful (with wisdom realization),
more learned (than you), enthusiastic (to help others),
well versed (in the three divisions of scriptures).
Having realized the true nature, skilled in teaching,
Kind (in teaching), and indefatigable (in teaching).[6]

Therefore, what you are looking for is the true Dharma qualities in teachers without getting fooled by some impressive orchestration of high titles, wealth, charisma, influence, good looks, and smooth discourse, any of which might make you distracted from your precious path. Paltrul Rinpoche writes,

For the teachers, the only important qualities that they must have are compassion and the realization of the view. You should not judge them on the basis of whether they are skilled in pretending or in talking; nor on whether they have high designations, or the titles of tulkus, or possess hordes of horses and mules, or are enjoying fancy encampment facilities, or have attractive looks, or gaze around charmingly.[7]

However, even if you are unable to find teachers who have realizations of any high wisdom or all of the qualities listed in the teachings, if their hearts are pure and kind, their actions are clean and transparent, and the knowledge that they are sharing is true Dharma, then they are qualified to be teachers, because finding people who enjoy all the ten qualities— especially having the high realization of wisdom—is rare in this age. Here is a story that exemplifies this: Even at the time of the Buddha, a disciple of his went to a far-distant land. He taught meditations that he had learned from the Buddha. As a result of this a number of his students became realized sages (Skt., *arhat*), even though the teacher himself hadn't yet become a sage. So if you receive the correct teachings, you could get the highest benefits.

9. What is the significance of the Tibetan terms "Rinpoche, or Rinpoche La," "Tulku, or Tulku La," "Khenpo, or Khenpo La"?

Tulku and Khenpo are titles with special significance. Tulku is the title exclusively for the rebirths of deceased high lamas, as we have discussed. Khenpo is the title exclusively for the senior monks and the heads of the monastic communities who have been ordained for ten years[8] or more and are observing monastic[9] rules, including celibacy.

Rinpoche means "the Precious One." It is one of the highest honorific terms that you can find in Tibetan, and is used for addressing the highest lamas. You can use Rinpoche by adding it after the titles of the lamas or using it independently, as, Tulku Rinpoche for tulkus, Khen Rinpoche for khenpos, or just Rinpoche for both.

When it comes to using "La," you must consider the geographical background of the person you are addressing. If they are from Central Tibet and if they are equal to you or only a little higher than you, then you add "La" after the title—for example, Tulku La or Khenpo La. If they are higher than you, you should not use "La," but address them as Tulku Rinpoche or just Rinpoche, Khen Rinpoche or just Rinpoche. So, keep in mind, that if you are addressing a tulku, khenpo, or rinpoche who is higher than you and if you add "La" after their titles, it may come across as patronizing.

If they are from Kham or Amdo provinces, you don't add "La" at all after their titles or names. You just address them as Tulku, Khenpo, or Rinpoche.

10. Even if we are not seeing or hearing them, can tulkus still be benefiting us?

Most of the time, tulkus will be able to serve others, both directly and indirectly. They may be benefiting many by teaching and working with people directly in monasteries or

in towns, or they may be doing meditations and prayers for all
beings in a cave alone in seclusion. Either way, the degree of
their effectiveness depends on two factors—the level of their
own enlightened power and the karmic openness of the beings
to whom they are offering their service.

11. If you become a tulku, will you always remain a tulku?

Even if lamas are real tulkus of virtuous lamas, unless they
have reached higher stages of attainments, they must work hard
at their studies, trainings, and attainments. If they don't, as
we discussed earlier, they might gradually fall by exhausting
what spiritual attainments they had accomplished in the past,
because elementary attainments are reversible.

*12. The tulkus of virtuous lamas are still under karmic conditions,
but why do tulkus of buddhas and adepts have to study hard, suffer
badly, and end in death the way ordinary people do?*

Because they have taken the forms of ordinary beings in
order to reach and serve ordinary beings and to suit their perceptions and culture. As long as tulkus have taken gross forms,
they will follow the laws of gross phenomena. Even if they
appear to be suffering, that is at the level of appearances and for
a purpose and is not so in reality.

If they can reach others more easily through the forms of
ordinary beings, then they must appear this way, since their
aspirations and purpose are to reach and serve others in the
easiest and best way. For example, if you wish to communicate
with children, you have to think and talk like a child.

Tulkus in general and especially tulkus of buddhas and
adepts, naturally enjoy extraordinary wisdom and miracles,
as have been manifested and recorded throughout Buddhist
history. But many do appear and function in very simple and
ordinary appearances and culture. For example, gold always
remains pure and precious, but if the gold is in the form of a

spoon, it will scoop the soup. If it is in the form of a crown, it will adorn the head of the lord.

13. If buddhas transcend worldly existence, how can they appear in this world?

Buddhas never appear or remain in the mundane world after their *mahaparinirvana,* but their infinite tulkus, the reflection-like manifestations, will keep appearing in the world because of their love and enlightened aspirations and they will keep serving all of those who are open. Santideva explains with an example that if a healer has created a medicinal plant, then that plant will keep curing people even long after the healer is dead. In the same way, even though a person who has attained buddhahood is no longer in the mundane world, his or her tulkus will keep appearing as long as there are beings who are open to his or her service because of the power of past aspirations and the unconditional love of the Buddha, which is omnipresent. Santideva writes,[10]

If a healer dies after creating a (healing) monument
   of Garuda,[11]
The monument will keep curing toxicities for a long
   time even after his death.
Likewise, if a bodhisattva accomplishes the
   monument-like
Buddhahood through the bodhisattva trainings,
The bodhisattva will keep fulfilling the needs
   (of beings),
Even if he has attained nirvana.

How to Become and Function
as a Tulku

ANYONE CAN BECOME A TULKU

Any person can become a tulku if he or she earnestly pursues
Dharma trainings. Even if individual lamas are not real tulkus,
if they are trained earnestly and remain on their spiritual path
by studying and training consistently, they will become the
sources of great benefits as tulkus. Then they may progress
through different levels of tulkuhood if they wish, and if they
keep their spiritual journey intact.

As we discussed, everyone has buddha-nature, so everyone has the possibility of realizing it and becoming a tulku.
For those who are totally devout in Dharma training, there is
the possibility of attaining not only tulkuhood but buddhahood in one lifetime. Then they can manifest as infinite tulkus
whenever needed, and appear as the manifestation-bodies of
the Buddha in this very lifetime as well as in the future. Or
in the case of those who become highly accomplished adepts,
they can manifest tulkus of the adepts in order to benefit many
in this lifetime as well as in the future. For those who are able
to accumulate a great amount of meritorious deeds, their rebirths could become the tulkus of virtuous lamas—sources
of dual benefits. Such tulkus may or may not be recognized
as tulkus, but they will function as tulkus and benefit many.
Therefore, tulkuhood is not reserved for some special class of

people; rather, we all have the quality and ability to realize and manifest this.

As discussed in relation to the four foundations of tulkus, beings must first develop the enlightened aspirations by which they commit themselves to serving all with pure love and compassion. By means of meditation and enlightening aspirations and actions, and thus accumulating merit, they will produce positive karma. At that point they might even go beyond karmic conditions by realizing the wisdom of openness (emptiness). As a result, they might attain the three buddhabodies—the true nature and qualities of all beings—and serve many through their various manifestations. Or they could benefit many by becoming the tulkus of virtuous lamas.

STARTING ON THE PATH TO TULKUHOOD

The most important means to becoming a tulku or a buddha is through meditation. There are thousands of different meditations in the Tibetan Buddhist tradition. Here, just as a simple example, I am offering a brief outline of the meditation on loving-kindness.[1] In this meditation, we are opening our heart and transforming our life with loving-kindness, "wishing joy for all." We can generate loving-kindness in ourselves in many ways, but we practice it here through the power of positive perception, devotional prayers and meditation, and pure love for all. Such meditation might progress through the following three stages.

First, visualize, think, feel, and trust, without any hesitation, that you are in the presence of the Buddha of Loving-kindness or Compassion, who is[2] in front of you. His body is a body of pure radiant and colorful light, and his mind is filled with all-knowing wisdom and unconditional love. Then with the pure love of wishing joy for all beings and total devotion of joy and trust—openness to the Buddha without any hesitation—pray by singing, OM MANI PADME HUNG (pronounced "hoong").

Pray by singing, hearing, and feeling the sounds of the waves of the energy of love and devotion. By praying in such a way, you open yourself fully to enjoy the pure image of the light of love, or the positive feelings of unconditional love and the energy of total trust in the Buddha's presence and qualities. The qualities of your mind and life always change with how you react to what you see and what you think about it and how you open and let it reflect in you.

As the result, see that from the Buddha infinite beams come to you of the blessing light of his unconditional love warmed by blissful heat. They fill you and transform your body into a body of blessing light and your mind into a mind of unconditional, universal, and pure love. You have become free from the confinements of rigid mentality, grasping tightness, afflicting emotions, harsh sensations, as well as from a rigid and gross body.

Second, as soon as you are seeing and feeling Buddha's unconditional love and his body of light from the depth of your heart and enjoying his blessings, you will find that your mind has been transformed into a mind of boundless and openness wisdom and unconditional love. Now, the love of the Buddha as well as the Buddha himself is not somewhere else, but in you—as you.

Recognize and enjoy your own great transformation, and pray. Pray by singing, hearing and feeling the sounds and the waves of the energy of unconditional love that are opening and expanding your body of light and mind of love of the Buddha of Loving-kindness toward all, wherever your mind goes.

Finally, when you are finding such light, love, and wisdom in yourself, at that moment whatever you see, hear, and feel—all will become the awareness of images, sounds, and feelings of unconditional love and openness wisdom. Enjoying such awareness, pray again. At the end, enjoy the boundless love, and just rest in the awareness of that universal love as one.

Such meditation, if you do it earnestly, accomplishes the trainings of all the six perfections that condense the essence of all the mahayana trainings. The six perfections are generosity, moral discipline, tolerance, diligence, tranquillity, and wisdom. Meditation on loving-kindness in which there is no grasping at "self" or attachment is generosity. Treating all with true loving-kindness is moral discipline. Maintaining loving-kindness to all without hesitation is patience. Maintaining loving-kindness with total joy is diligence. Remaining in loving-kindness with no wavering is contemplation. The realization of the true nature, the union of loving-kindness and openness (emptiness) wisdom is the wisdom. Therefore, Jetsun Milarepa says,

> There is no giving, but letting go of the grasping at self.
> There is no moral discipline, but letting go of deceptions.
> There is no patience, but fearlessness of truth.
> There is no diligence, but inseparability from the
>   trainings.
> There is no contemplation, but remaining in the nature.
> There is no wisdom, but the realization of the true
>   nature.[3]

Also, as soon you realize wisdom—the openness (emptiness) nature—you instantly develop unconditional love and compassion. Then you will spontaneously be able to serve all with the power of your enlightened aspirations. Jigme Lingpa writes,

> When you realize emptiness, it is impossible not to
>   develop compassion.
> If you have compassion, beneficial service for others will
>   take place spontaneously.
> Only the adepts who have realized the truth
> Have the realization of the enlightened aspiration free
>   from concepts, but no one else.[4]

Also through the trainings on the first five perfections, you accomplish the accumulation of merits. Through the sixth perfection, you accomplish the accumulation of wisdom. Through the accomplishments of the dual accumulations—merit and wisdom—buddhahood will be realized. Nagarjuna writes,

> The realization of the form-bodies[5] of the Buddha
> Is caused by the accumulation of merit.
> The ultimate-body is caused
> By the accumulation of the supreme wisdom.
> So, these two accumulations are
> The causes of attaining the very buddhahood.[6]

Therefore, the right meditations and beneficial actions will lead us to discover our own true buddha-nature and qualities. That will enable us to serve others as the tulkus of the buddhas or of the adepts. Because of lack of meditative strength, even if we couldn't reach such high attainments, such meditations will help us to ease the predicaments of life and to lead us toward a more peaceful, joyful, and beneficial state of life. Our lives will naturally become healthier and more spiritual. Then our rebirths will become the sources of true peace, joy, and love for many—true tulkus of virtuous lamas.

So, the idea of awakening one's own tulku qualities and serving others through such gifts is not a foreign concept or one reserved to benefit a particular group of people. It is the natural progression through which anyone can realize his or her own inherited potential and express it and serve others through the same universal skills and wisdom.

THE FOUR MAJOR TASKS THAT TULKUS MUST FULFILL

The main goal of the lives of tulkus is to serve beings and the Dharma. But in order to equip themselves for such a task and to teach and serve their followers, tulkus must fulfill four major traditional tasks as a curriculum—learning, training, at-tainments, and service. Tulkus must learn the teachings, train in what they have learned through meditation, and attain the realizations in order to serve all. Vasubandhu writes,

> There are two aspects to the holy Dharma of the Buddha.
> They are the teachings and the realizations.
> Uphold the teachings by learning and by teaching, and
>   the realizations by training in them.[7]

Studies

Tulkus must start learning the teachings—on philosophical views, meditation practices, and benefiting others with ser-vice—through studying, debating, and doing research on the teachings at the feet of learned teachers in the sanctuaries of scholastic institutions. Without studying, no one will know what Dharma is. Without knowing the Dharma, even if you try to meditate, you will hardly attain any fruition, since you might be on the wrong track even without knowing it.

Therefore, tulkus usually start their studies, in private or in groups, at the age of four or five, and might continue, for the next twenty years or more, to dedicate most of their waking hours to study, seven days a week.

Trainings

After the completion of their general studies, tulkus must train in the teachings that they have studied by doing meditations, reciting prayers, performing ritual ceremonies in groups or in solitary retreats, and performing services for others who are in need and are open. These trainings are for perfecting the two accumulations—the accumulations of meritorious deeds and the realization of the wisdom of openness (emptiness).

Generally, trainings will last until the attainment of buddha-hood, but tulkus must spend years, at the very least, exclusively at their trainings. Trainings will result in various spiritual attainments, which are the heart and goal of the Dharma and the Dharma life. Without meditation trainings, learning will bear few Dharma fruits to enjoy or share with others.

Attainments

As the results of the training in various meditations and Dharma activities, a person can attain two levels of accomplishments. At the level of the common accomplishments, one can enjoy peace, joy, prosperity, good health, miraculous powers, and knowledge. At the level of the supreme accomplishments, one may attain various stages of enlightenment, the very highest of which is the attainment of the fully enlightened state, buddhahood.

Some tulkus may not need to go through learning, training, or attainments, as they may already have perfected them in their past lives, but they pursue them anyway in order to teach their followers and to show a good example of what students must do.

Services for Others

Serving others is the natural gift and the purpose of the trainings on the Dharma path. There are four ways of serving or gathering others to the Dharma.[8] They are (a) welcoming others to the Dharma with gifts of materials, teachings, and protection;[9] (b) bringing others to the Dharma with kind words and inspiring teachings that suit them; (c) leading others to different levels of Dharma trainings in accordance with their capacities and needs; and (d) observing the same trainings and disciplines oneself that one is teaching others so that one becomes an example of true Dharma spirit and dedication for others.[10]

Beginning in their forties or so, tulkus usually start serving others for the rest of their lives by teaching, praying and offering what they have realized. Because of the skill of their knowledge and the power of their attainments, they will not only help others to learn the teachings but will also help them to realize their own buddha-nature and buddha-qualities— the ultimate peace, joy, and wisdom—since every being possesses them.

The obligations of true tulkus is to dedicate their total life forever in the beneficial service of others in the forms of buddha-manifestations, bodhisattvas, adepts, or virtuous teachers through various means and actions with unconditional love and wisdom, without even a trace of selfishness. That is the true path and the goal aspired to by tulkus, for which the great bodhisattva Santideva prayed:

> For as long as space exists,
> For as long as beings exist,
> May I too remain in this world
> To dispel the miseries of all.[11]

GLOSSARY

ADEPT. A highly realized master—either the bodhisattva ("seeker of full enlightenment") of exoteric Buddhism, or the siddha ("highly accomplished one") of esoteric Buddhism.

ANANDA. Sakyamuni Buddha's first cousin, one of his foremost disciples, and his constant attendant for his last twenty-five years.

ARTISAN MANIFESTED-BODY (Skt., *silpin nirmanakaya;* Tib., *bzo sprul sku*). One of the four kinds of manifested-bodies of the Buddha.

ASANGA (fourth century). One of the two greatest scholars and writers of the Mahayana Buddhist tradition and the founder of the Mind Only school.

ATISA (980–1054). A great bodhisattva and scholar from Vikramasila Monastery in Bengal, India, who invigorated and refined Buddhism in Tibet. His chief disciple, Dromton, founded the Kadam school.

AVALOKITESVARA (Tib., *spyan ras gzigs*). Also known as the Buddha of Loving-Kindness or the Buddha of Compassion. In meditations he is an object of prayer with devotion, a source of blessings, and the means of transforming oneself into the mind and actions of loving-kindness.

BARDO (Tib., *bar do*). The "intermediate state," the period between death and rebirth that every being travels through after death.

BIRTH MANIFESTED-BODY (Skt., *janma-nirmanakaya;* Tib., *skye ba sprul sku*). One of the four manifested-bodies of the Buddha taking the forms of ordinary beings. This is the main basis of the tulku tradition of Tibetan Buddhists.

BLESSED TULKU (Tib., *byin gyis brlabs pa'i sprul sku*). A tulku who is not the actual rebirth of the identified deceased lama, but is recognized as the tulku so that he or she can serve others on behalf of the deceased lama.

BODHICITTA (Tib., *byang ch'ub kyi sems*). Enlightened aspiration, the intention or aspiration for all to become buddhas and the vow to lead all to peace, joy, and buddhahood.

BODHISATTVA (Tib., *byang ch'ub sems dpa'*). The "seeker of enlightenment," one who has developed bodhicitta, the vow to lead all beings to happiness and enlightenment without self-interest.

BUDDHA. A fully enlightened one or fully enlightened state. According to Buddhism, it is the ultimate nature and qualities of all. Full enlightenment consists of attaining three Buddha bodies (dharmakaya, sambhogakaya, and nirmanakaya) and it is the ultimate goal of Buddhist training. The term *buddha* can be singular or plural. To indicate the absolute Buddha, which is the unity of all, *Buddha* is used in the singular. To indicate the manifestations of Buddha, which are infinite, the plural is used.

BUDDHA OF LOVING-KINDNESS. See Avalokitesvara.

BUDDHA SAKYAMUNI. The name of the historical Buddha. He is also known as Gautama Buddha or the Buddha.

DALAI LAMA. The most important tulku lineage in Tibet. The present Dalai Lama is the fourteenth.

DIVERSE MANIFESTED-BODY (Tib., *sna tshogs sprul sku*). One of the four kinds of manifested bodies of the buddhas that appear in various forms.

ENJOYMENT-BODY (Skt., *sambhogakaya;* Tib., *longs sku*). One of the three bodies or aspects of buddhahood; the subtlest form-body.

ENLIGHTENED ASPIRATION. See bodhicitta.

FINAL FIVE-HUNDRED-YEAR PERIOD. The last five hundred years of the five thousand years of Buddhism's expected life. It is a synonym for the degeneration of Buddhism.

FOUR WAYS OF GATHERING OTHERS (Skt., *samgraha-vastu;* Tib., *bsdu ba rnam pa bzhi*). The four ways through which the bodhisattvas bring others to the Dharma.

FIVE BUDDHA-FAMILIES OR BUDDHA LINEAGES (Skt., *pancabuddhakula;* Tib., *rgyal ba rigs lnga*). It is the state of being, in all phenomena—physical and mental, as the union of the five male buddhas and the five female buddhas.

FIVE CERTAINTIES (Tib., *nges pa lnga ldan*). The five everlasting and never-changing qualities of the enjoyment-body of buddhahood: (1) the place is self-appearing or self-present, free from dimensions; (2) the teachers are the Buddhas of the five classes or families; (3) the disciples are infinite and inseparable from the teacher; (4) the teachings are great luminescent vision, ineffable beyond concepts or words; (5) the time is changeless and timeless time.

FIVEFOLD-WISDOM (Skt., *pancajnana;* Tib., *ye shes lnga*). The fivefold-wisdom of buddhahood: (1) the Wisdom of the Ultimate Sphere; (2) the Mirror-like Wisdom; (3) the Wisdom of Equanimity; (4) the Distinguishing (or All-knowing) Wisdom; (5) the Wisdom of Accomplishment.

FALLEN TULKU (Tib., *sprul rgod or sprul log*). A tulku who has ceased to remain as a tulku.

FALSE TULKU (Tib., *sprul rdzun*). One who has never been a tulku and has been designated as such falsely or by mistake.

GARUDA (Tib., *khyung*). A mystical bird.

GELUG. One of the four major Buddhist schools of Tibet. It was founded by Je Tsongkhapa.

KADAM. An important school, founded by Dromtonpa, the chief disciple of Atisa. Later, the Kadam teachings were disseminated and absorbed into the teachings of other schools.

KAGYU. One of the four major Buddhist schools of Tibet, founded by Marpa Chökyi Lodrö.

KARMA. A habitual pattern sown in our mind-stream by our thoughts and deeds. Such karmic patterns determine what kind of life experiences we will have in the future.

KARMAPA. One of the most important tulku lineages of Tibet. The present one is the seventeenth in the tulku lineage of Karmapas.

KHENPO (Tib., *mkhan po;* Skt., *upadhyaya*). An abbot; a designation of senior monks, whose roles are detailed in the *vinaya* scriptures of Buddhism.

KING TRISONG DETSEN. A great king of Tibet, who was responsible for establishing Buddhism in Tibet in the ninth century.

KOR (Tib., *dkor*). Materials and services dedicated for Dharma purposes.

LAMA (Tib., *bla ma;* Skt., *guru*). One of the "superior ones"; a senior teacher of Buddhism.

LOVING-KINDNESS (Skt., *maitri;* Tib., *byams pa*). The thought of wishing joy and enlightenment for all.

MAHAPARINIRVANA. Literally, "going beyond suffering"; the death of the Buddha or of any highly realized tulku or lama.

MAHAYANA. One of the two major divisions of Buddhism—Mahayana means "the Great Vehicle," and Hinayana means "the Common Vehicle."

MANIFESTED-BODY (Skt., *nirmanakaya;* Tib., *sprul sku*). One of the three bodies of the Buddha, the one that appears in ordinary forms so that it can be seen by ordinary beings. In Tibetan this is called *tulku.*

NAGARJUNA (first to second century?). The preeminent proponent of emptiness philosophy of Mahayana Buddhism and the founder of the Middle Way.

NALANDA MONASTERY. One of the greatest academic institutes of the ancient mahayana tradition of India. Its ruins can be found in Bihar State of modern India.

NYINGMA. Literally, "the Ancient One"; one of the four major Buddhist schools of Tibet, founded by Guru Padmasambhava in the ninth century.

OPENNESS. A translation of the Sanskrit word *shunyata,* which is a philosophical term that is often translated as emptiness. Openness denotes the unrestricted, uncontrived, unbounded, unhindered, nondual, unchanging, and fully-awakened state, Buddhahood.

PADMASAMBHAVA. Also known as Guru Rinpoche. One of the greatest adepts of India, who founded Buddhism in Tibet in the ninth century.

PATH (Skt., *marga;* Tib., *lam*). In Mahayana Buddhism, one progresses through five paths and ten stages of training in order to attain buddhahood.

PURE LAND (Skt. *Buddhaksetra;* Tib., *zhing khams* or *dag pa'i zhing khams*). A buddha paradise. There are two levels of pure lands: the pure land that belongs to the manifested-body of the Buddha, which can be seen by ordinary beings; and the pure land of the enjoyment-body of the buddhas.

RAINBOW BODY (Tib., *'ja' lus*). Some adepts totally dissolve their gross/mortal bodies at the time of their death, leaving only the nails and hair behind. This dissolution is called "the attainment of rainbow-body" since while their bodies totally dissolve, a mass of rainbow-lights in the form of beams and circles, and especially spheres of light (Tib., *thigle*) appear for days.

RAINBOW BODY OF GREAT TRANSFERENCE (Tib., *'ja' lus 'pho ba ch'en po*). The subtle body of light into which a great adept transforms his or her gross body in order to serve others.

REBIRTH. What eventually occurs after one's death, which is not the end of one's existence. Again and again, after each death, one's mind, the consciousness, takes rebirth as another being.

REBIRTHS OF VIRTUOUS LAMAS. See Virtuous lama.

RECOGNITION. The term used in Tibet for the way realized lamas identify the rebirths of deceased lamas through their clairvoyance and spiritual power.

RENUNCIATE (Skt., *pravrajika;* Tib., *rab byung*). One who has renounced household life and lives as an ascetic or a celibate monk or nun.

RETURNER FROM DEATH (Tib. *'das log*). A person who has died and then, after a number of days, returned to life with vivid memories of his or her after-death experiences. A phenomenon known for centuries in Tibet and reported by many.

RINGSEL (Tib., *ring-bsrel;* Skt., *sarira*). Highly respected sacred relics materialized from the cremated bones of highly accomplished masters. They are pellets that might look like small pearls, hard and shiny; they are mostly white, but they could also be in various colors. Ringsels are produced from the cremated bones of meditators and they are believed to be great signs of their high realization.

SAKYA. One of the four major Buddhist schools of Tibet, founded by Khon Könchok Gyalpo.

SANGHA (Tib., *dge 'dun*). Dharma communities: the communities of monks, nuns, tantrikas, or devotees.

SEEKER OF ENLIGHTENMENT FOR ALL. See bodhisattva.

SIDDHA. A highly accomplished master who has reached high attainment through trainings in the esoteric teachings of Buddhism.

SIXTY ASPECTS OF MELODIOUS VOICE. The various wondrous qualities of the speech and voice of the Buddha.

SANTARAKSITA (ninth century). A great mahayana scholar of ancient India, who established the monastic ordination lineage in Tibet.

STAGES (Skt., *bhumi;* Tib., *sa*). According to Mahayana Buddhism, one must advance through ten stages and five paths to reach the goal, buddhahood.

SUPREME MANIFESTED-BODY (Skt., *uttama-nirmanakaya;* Tib., *mch'og gi sprul sku*). The supreme among the four classes of the manifested-bodies of the Buddha that appear in ordinary forms, such as the historical Buddha.

SUTRA (Tib., *mdo*). The exoteric, common teachings of Buddhism taught by the historical Buddha himself.

TATHAGATA. Literally, "such gone"; an epithet of the Buddha.

TANTRA (Tib., *sngags*). The esoteric or uncommon teachings of Buddhism taught by the historical Buddha or other buddhas.

TANTRIKA (Tib., *sngags pa*). A follower of esoteric teachings, the tantra.

TER or TERMA (Tib., *gter* or *gter ma*). Literally, "the treasured or hidden ones." Unique esoteric teachings concealed and discovered through enlightened power. In Tibet, most of them were concealed by Guru Padmasambhava in the ninth century and discovered by the tulkus of his disciples starting in the eleventh century and continuing until today.

TERTÖN (Tib., *gter ston*). Literally, "treasure discoverer." A master who discovers the ter teachings through his or her enlightened mystical power.

THIGLE (Tib., *thig le*). The Tibetan word *thigle* generally means a circle, sphere, disc, or drop. However, in the context of *thigle* of light in esoteric teachings such as Dzogchen, it is a sphere of rainbow light—small or big—made of single or multiple colors. *Thigles* are neither the beams nor the empty circles made of rainbow-like lights, but are spheres of colorful light fully filled with light. Highly accomplished meditators might see them as Buddha images or might see Buddha images inside them. *Thigles* are one of the signs that the particles of the physical body of the deceased meditator have been, or are being, transformed into pure light in order to unite with the mother luminous light of wisdom, the ultimate pure body of Buddhahood, which ordinary eyes cannot see as it is.

THIRTY-TWO MAJOR AND EIGHTY MINOR EXCELLENT MARKS. The 112 extraordinary physical attributes of the supreme manifested-body, such as the historical Buddha.

THREE BUDDHA-BODIES (Skt., *trikaya;* Tib., *sku gsum*). The ultimate-body, the enjoyment-body, and the manifested-body of the Buddha.

TULKU (Tib., *sprul sku;* Skt., *nirmanakaya*). The manifested-body. One of the three bodies of the Buddha. In Tibetan tradition, however, we find three divisions within tulku itself: the tulkus of the Buddha, the tulkus of the adepts, and the tulkus of the virtuous or meritorious lamas.

TUSITA HEAVEN (Tib., *dga' ldan*). One of the six heavenly fields of the desire realm.

ULTIMATE-BODY (Skt., *dharmakaya;* Tib., *ch'os sku*). One of the three bodies or aspects of buddhahood—the absolute and emptiness or openness nature of buddhahood and of all.

UNRECOGNIZED TULKU. One type of the infinite tulkus of buddhas and adepts, who, with the exception of a few, mostly remain unrecognized.

VIRTUOUS LAMA or **VIRTUOUS FRIEND** (Skt., *kalyanami-tra* or *guru;* Tib., *gde ba'i bshes gnyen* or *bla ma*). A teacher who has not yet attained the level of an adept or a buddha, but has generated virtuous deeds or meritorious karmas and whose rebirths will benefit many. Most of the tulkus of Tibet could belong to the rebirths of such lamas.

ZANGDOK PALRI (Tib., *zangs mdog dpal ri*), the Glorious Copper-colored Mountain. A manifested pure land, where Guru Padmasambhava remains in his rainbow body of great transference.

BIBLIOGRAPHY WITH
ABBREVIATIONS KEY

AFP   *Autobiography of the First Panchen Lama* (India: Ngawang Geleg Demo, 1969).

BDT   *Biographical Dictionary of Tibet and Tibetan Buddhism,* by Khetsun Zangpo, vol. 4 (Dharamsala, India: Library of Tibetan Works and Archives, 1973).

BLC   *Byang ch'ub lam rim ch'e ba,* by Tsongkhapa (Taiwan: The Corporate Body of the Buddha Educational Foundation [TCBBEF], 1990).

BM   *Brilliant Moon: The Autobiography of Dilgo Khyentse,* trans. Ani Jinba Palmo (Boston: Shambhala, 2008).

BMT   *Bhota'i yul gyi slob dpon ch'en po Manjusrimitra'i rtogs brjod 'jig rten kun tu dga' ba'i gter,* by Jigme Tenpe Nyima. Dodrupchen Sungbum, vol. 5 (China: Sitron Mirig, 2003).

BS   *Blazing Splendor: The Memoirs of Tulku Urgyen Rinpoche,* as told to Erik Pema Kunzang and Marcia Binder Schmidt (Boudhanath, Hong Kong, and Esby: Rangjung Yeshe, 2005).

BSK   Biography of Sera Khandro, by Sarah Jacoby (Rigpa Wiki, n.d.).

BSP   *Byang ch'ub sems dpa'i spyod pa la 'jug pa,* by Santideva (Tibet: Dodrupchen Gon Wooden Block Print, n.d.).

BT   *Born in Tibet,* by Chögyam Trungpa (Boulder: Shambhala, 1977).

BTT   *dBu ma rtsa ba'i tshigs le-ur byas pa shes rab,* by Nagarjuna (Taiwan: TCBBEF, 1990).

CND   *Ch'os mngon pa'i mdzod,* by Vasubandhu (China: Sitron Mirig, 1996).

CT   *Chögyam Trungpa: His Life and Vision,* by Fabrice Midal (Boston: Shambhala, 2004).

DC   *Dbus mo bde ba'i rdo rje'i rnam par thar pa nges 'byung 'dren pa'i shing rta skal ldan dad pa'i mchod sdong* (the autobiography of Sera Khandro Dewe Dorje) (China: Sitron Mirig Petrunkhang, n.d.).

DD   *rJe btsun mi 'gyur dpal gyi sgron ma'i rnam thar dad pa'i gdung sel,* by Repa Gyurme Odsal (Bhutan: National Library of Bhutan, 1984). TBRC W23846.

DDG   *Theg pa ch'en po mdo sde'i rgyan,* by Asanga. Jamcho De-nga'i Tsawa (Taiwan: TCBBEF, 1990).

DK   *Drang srong skyo glu nyes pa'i mtshangs 'don,* by Khenpo Ngawang Palzang. Sungbum, vol. 2. (Publisher unknown, n.d., p. 194).

DKN   *rDo grub ch'en sku phreng rnam bzha'i rnam thar,* by the Fourth Dodrupchen (Delhi: Pema Thinley, 2000).

DN   *Deb ther sngon po,* by Gölo Zhunnu Pal (China: Sitron Mirig, 1984).

DND   *dBus bza mkha' 'gro'i 'das rjes kyi rnam thar don bsdus,* by Tshulthrim Dorje (China: Sitron Mirig Petrunkhang, n.d.).

DR   *gSar rnying gi gdan rabs mdor bsdud,* by Khyentse'i Wangpo. Khyentse'i Sungbum Thorbu (China: Sitron Mirig, 1989).

DSD   *Thabs la mkhas pa drin lan bsab pa'i mdo.* Dode, vol. Aha, Kajur (Tibet: Dege Edition, n.d.).

DSR   *sDom pa gsum gyi rab tu dbye ba,* by Kunga Gyaltsen Palzangpo. Sakya'i Kabum, vol. Na (Dehradun, India: Sakya Center, 1993). TBRC W22271.

DTC   *Shes rab kyi pha rol du phyin pa sdud pa tshigs su bchad pa.* Sherab Natshog, vol. Ka, Kajur (Tibet: Dege Edition, n.d.).

GB   *Theg pa ch'en po rgyud bla ma,* by Asanga (China: Sitron Mirig, 1995).

GLS   *rGyals sras lag len so bdun ma,* by Thogme Zangpo (unpublished manuscript).

GNT   *dGe slong gi bslab bya gnam rtsed ldeng ma,* by Tsongkhapa. Je'i Sungbum, vol. Ka (Tibet: Lhasa Zhol Edition, n.d.). TBRC W635.

GS   *sDom pa gsum gyi rab du dbye ba'i rnam bshad rgyal ba'i gsung rab kyi dgongs pa gsal ba,* by Sodnam Senge. Sungbum, vol. 9 (Dehradun, India: Sakya College, 1979).

GSM   *Grub mtha' shel gyi me long,* by Thukvan Chökyi Nyima (India: Ngawang Geleg Demo, n.d.).

GTN *rGyal sras thogs med rin po ch'e'i rnam thar dad pa'i gsal 'debs,*
     by Zhonu Gyaltshen (China: Paltseg Edition, Bojong Mirig,
     2008).

GTR *rGyal po la gtam bya ba rin po ch'e'i phreng ba,* by Nagarjuna.
     Uma Rigtshog Drug (Taiwan: TCBBEF, 1990).

HPLK *The Healing Power of Loving-Kindness,* by Tulku Thondup
     (Boston: Shambhala, 2009).

HSK *The History of the Sixteen Karmapas of Tibet,* by Karma Thinley
     (Boulder: Prajna, 1980).

HTT *Hidden Teachings of Tibet,* by Tulku Thondup Rinpoche, ed.
     Harold Talbott. (Boston: Wisdom, 1986).

JKS *Rig 'dzin 'jigs med gling pa'i 'khrung rabs gsol 'deb,* by Jigme
     Lingpa. Long-nying Doncha, vol. 2 (India: Sikkim, n.d.).

JKT *'Jam dbyangs mkhyen brtse'i dbang po'i rtogs brjod,* by Jigme
     Tenpe Nyima. Dodrupchen Sungbum, vol. 5 (China: Sitron
     Mirig, 2003).

JN   *rJe btsun thams chad mkhyen pa'i gsung 'bum thor bu las rje
     nyid kyi rnam thar,* by Gedun Gyatsho. Gedun Gyatsho'i
     Sungbum, vol. Ka (India: LTWA, 2006). TBRC W1CZ2857.

JSN *rJe rin po ch'e'i gsang ba'i rnam thar rin po ch'e'i snye ma,* by
     Geleg Palzangpo. Je'i Sungbum, vol. Ka (Tibet: Kubum Wood
     Block Print, n.d.). TBRC W2272.

KBZ *sNgon 'gro'i khrid yig kun bzang bla ma'i zhal lung,* by Paltrul
     Rinpoche (China: Sitron Mirig, 1988).

KG   *mKhas pa'i dga' ston,* by Pawo Tsuglag Threngwa (China:
     Mirig, 1985).

KJ   *mKhas pa'i tshul la 'jug pa'i sgo,* by Mipham Jamyang Namgyal
     (China: Sitron Mirig, 1990).

KJD *mKhas 'jug gi sdom byang,* by Mipham Jamyang Gyepa (China:
     Sitron Mirig, 1990).

KKN *Karmapa sku 'phreng rim byon gyi rnam thar mdor bsdus dpag
     bsam 'khri shing,* by Karma Ngedon Tengye. Ngedon Tengye
     Sungbum, vol. Kha (India: Bir, 1976). TBRC: W10982.

KN   *sKu stod kyi rnam thar zhal gsung ma* (The autobiography of
     Dilgo Khyentse Rinpoche). Dilgo Khyentse'i Sungbum, vol.
     7 (India: Shechen Edition, 1994).

KNT *Rang rnam tshigs bcad ma ku su la'i nyams byung gi gtam*
     (autobiography) by Dekyong Chonyi Wangmo (China:
     Sichuan Petrun Tsogpa, 2009).

KP   *sKye 'phreng by Kunzang Zhenphen.* Long-nying Doncha
        Nyipa (India: Choten Gonpa, Sikkim, 1991).

KS   *'Phags pa sku gsum zhes bya ba.* Dode, vol.Ya, Kajur (Tibet:
        Dege Edition, n.d.).

KSN   *Kun mkhyen bsod nams seng ge'i rnam thar,* by Kong-ton (India:
        Trehor Dongthog, 1973).

KZ   *'Ja' lus rdo rje'i rnam thar mkha' 'gro'i zhal lung* (the
        autobiography of Do Khyentse) (China: Sitron Mirig,
        1997).

KZZ   *Kun bzang bla ma'i zhal lung gi zin bris,* by Pema Ledreltsal
        (China: Sitron Mirig, 1996).

LA   A Letter of Advice, by Lauthang Tulku Drachen (unpublished
        manuscript).

LKG   *Lung bstan bka' rgya ma,* discovered by Sangye Lingpa (India:
        Sherab Gyaltsen Lama, 1983) TBRC:W23433.

LLP   *Lives of the Teachers of Lam Rim Precepts,* by Tshechog Ling
        Yongdzin (India: Ngawang Geleg Demo, 1970).

LYN   *sNga 'gyur byung ba'i tshul lha dbang gyul las rgyal ba'i rnga bo
        ch'e'i sgra dbyangs,* by Jigdral Yeshey Dorje (India: Dudjom
        Tulku Rinpoche, 1967).

LW   *Light of Fearless Indestructible Wisdom,* by Khenpo Tsewang
        Dongyal (Ithaca, N.Y.: Snow Lion, 2008).

MGG   *A Marvelous Garland of Rare Gems,* by Nyoshul Khenpo
        (Junction City, California: Padma, 2005).

MK   *Bod mi bu gdong drug gi rus mdzod me tog skyed tshal,* by
        Kyilung Trashi Gyatsho (China:Tso-ngon Mirig, 1991).

ML   *The Mishap Lineage:Transcending Confusion into Wisdom,* by
        Chögyam Trungpa (Boston: Shambhala, 2009).

MLP   *My Land and My People: Memoirs of the Dalai Lama of Tibet*
        (New York: Potala Corporation, 1977).

MMM   *Masters of Meditation and Miracles,* by Tulku Thondup (Boston:
        Shambhala, 1996).

MN   *rJe btsun mi la ras pa'i rnam thar,* by Naljorpa Rüpe Gyenchen
        (China: n.d.).

MNT   *sGra bgyur mar pa lo tsa'i rnam thar mthong ba don yod,* by
        Thragthung Gyalpo (India: Palarampure, HP, 1976). TBRC
        W20499.

MRN   *rJe btsun mi la ras pa'i rnam thar rgyas par phye ba mgur 'bum,*
        by Jetsun Milarepa (India: Chitra Gon:Wooden Block Print,
        n.d.).

NB   *Gang shugs ma ni lo ch'en rig 'dzin dbang mo'i rnam thar*
        rnam khyen bde ster (the autobiography of Shugseb Lochen
        Chönyid Zangmo) (India: Reproduced by Sönam Kazi, n.d.).

NC   *sNyan rtsom gches btus,* by Paltrul Rinpoche (China: Sitron
        Mirig, 1992).

NG   *Ch'os mngon pa mdzod kyi 'grel ba mngon pa'i rgyan (mch'ims*
        ch'en), by Chim Jampeyang (India: Wooden Block Print,
        n.d.).

NGN   *mNyam med sgam po'i rnam par thar pa rin po ch'e'i rgyan,* by
        Sönam Lhundrup (China: Tso-ngon Mirig, 1993).

NLC   *rDzogs Pa Ch'en Po Nying Thig Gi Lo rGyus Ch'en Mo* (Vima
        Nyingthig, vol. 3), by Zhangton Tashi Dorje (Tibet: Adzom
        Edition).

NNG   *rGyal ba ka thog pa'i lo rgyus mdor bsdus Ngo mtshar rna ba'i dga'*
        ston, by Jamyang Gyaltshen (China: Sitron Mirig, 1990).

NNO   *Myang sprul sku Nyi ma od zer kyi rnam thar gsal ba'i me long,*
        by Nyang Lhundrup Ozer, Kagyed Desheg Düpa Collection,
        vol. Kha (Delhi: 1971). TBRC W22247.

NPDN   *Nyag bla padma bsud 'dul gyi rnam thar dang mgur 'bum,* by
        Yeshe Dorje (China: Sitron Mirig, 1998).

NTR   *sNga 'gyur ch'os kyi byung ba Ngo mtshar gtam gyi rol mtsho,* by
        Guru Trashi (China: Trungko Bodkyi Sherig, 1990).

NW   *Ngagyur Wodsel 1992* (periodical) (India: Ngagyur Nyingma
        Institute, Namdrolling, 1992).

PDJR   *Peaceful Death, Joyful Rebirth,* by Tulku Thondup (Boston:
        Shambhala, 2005).

PDN   *Pha dam pa sangs rgyas kyi rnam par thar pa dngos grub od stong*
        'bar ba'i nyi ma, by Chökyi Senge (China: Tso-ngon Mirig,
        1992).

PLT   *Padma las 'brel tsal gyi rtogs brjod ngo mtshar sgyu ma'i rol gar,* by
        Pema Ledreltsal (unpublished manuscript).

PST   *Pan ch'en thams chad mkhyen pa'i gsung thor bu,* by Panchen
        Sungbum, vol. 5 (Tibet: Tashi Lhunpo. Wooden Block Print,
        n.d.). TBRC W23430.

PT   *dPal sprul rin po ch'e'i rtogs brjod,* by Jigme Tenpe Nyima.
        Dodrupchen Sungbum, vol. 5 (China: Sitron Mirig, 2003).

RBP   *Zab mo'i gter dang gter ston ji ltar byon pa'i lo rgyus rin ch'en*
        baidurya'i phreng ba, by Kongtul Yonten Gyatso. *Rin chen gter*
        mdzod chen mo, vol. Ka (India: Shechen Publications, 2007/8),
        341–765. TBRC W1KG14.

RDN   *dPal ch'en rang byung rdo rje'i rnam thar.* Karmapa Rangjung
      Dorje'i Sungbum, vol. Nga (Tibet: Tsurphu Khenpo, 2006).
      TBRC W30541.

SN   *gSung ngag rin po che'i bla ma brgyud pa'i rnam thar glegs. Lam
      'bras slob bshad,* vol. 1 (Tibet: Dege Edition, n.d.).

TGS   *Thub pa'i dgongs pa rab tu gsal ba,* by Kunga Gyaltsen
      Palzangpo. Sakya Kabum, vol. Tha (Dehradun, India: Sakya
      Center, 1993). TBRC W22271.

TLP   *Lives of the Teachers of Lamrim Precepts,* by Yeshe Gyaltshen, vol.
      1 (India: Ngawang Gelek Demo, 1970).

TL   *The Treasury of Lives,* by Serah Jacoby (www.tibetanlineages.
      org).

TNN   *dPal rig 'dzin ch'en po tshe dbang nor bu zhabs kyi rnam thar
      ngo mtshar dad pa'i rol mtsho,* by Rigdzin Chökyi Wangchug.
      Tshewang Norbu'i Sungbum, vol. Ka (India: Damchoe
      Sangpo, 1976). TBRC W29688.

TPG   *'Phags pa thar pa ch'en po phyogs su rgyas pa.* Dode, vol. 'A,
      Kajur (Tibet: Dege Edition, n.d.).

TRG   *Thar pa rin po ch'e'i rgyan,* by Lhaje Sönam Rinchen (China:
      Sitron Mirig, 1989).

TRD   *Theg mch'og rin po ch'e'i mdzod,* by Ngagi Wangpo (Longchen
      Rabjam) (India: Reproduced by Dodrupchen Rinpoche,
      n.d.).

TT   *gTam tshogs,* by Jigme Lingpa. Sungbum of Jigme Lingpa, vol.
      Ja (Tibet: Adzom Edition, n.d.).

YN   *Rang byung rdo rje'i rnam par thar pa legs byas yongs 'dus snye ma*
      (the autobiography of Jigme Lingpa), vol. Ta, Jigling Kabum
      (India: Reproduced by Dodrupchen Rinpoche, n.d.).

YRD   *Yid bzhin rin po ch'e'i mdzod,* by Longchen Rabjam (Tibet:
      Adzom Edition, n.d.).

YSJ   *'Phags pa yab dang sras mjal ba. Kontseg,* vol. Nga, Kajur (Tibet:
      Dege Edition, n.d.).

ZS   *gTer ch'en ch'os kyi rgyal po khrag 'thung bdud 'joms gling pa'i
      rnam thar zhal gsung ma* (the autobiography of Dudjom
      Lingpa) (Tibet: a wooden block print, n.d.).

NOTES

Chapter 1: An Overview of the Three Types of Tulkus

1. (Skt., *nirmanakaya;* Tib., *sprul sku*).
2. Some modern Chinese secular translators seem to be rendering *tulku* as "soul boy" though in Buddhism there is no concept of "soul."
3. An adept is a bodhisattva (Tib., *byang ch'ub sems dpa'*) or siddha (Tib., *grub thob*); a highly accomplished master.
4. A learned religious teacher (Skt., *kalyanamitra* or *guru;* Tib., *gde ba'i bshes gnyen* or *bla ma*). The literal translation of *kalyanamitra* is "virtuous friend."
5. Reexistence. (Tib., *yang srid*).
6. Patrul Rinpoche, *The Words of My Perfect Teacher* (Boston: Shambhala Publications, p. 257).
7. (Skt., *riddhi* or *siddhi;* Tib., *rdzu 'phrul* or *grub rtags*).

Chapter 2: The History of the Tulku Tradition

1. NNO ff. 37a/3. In the bibliography, the titles of works cited are indicated by abbreviations, the key to which can be found in the reference. For instance, "BSP" stands for *Byang ch'ub sems dpa'i spyod pa la 'jug pa.* "ff" stands for "folio," the Tibetan style of pagination; and "p," for the western style of pagination. When paginations from traditional Tibetan are cited, the abbreviated title is followed by the folio number. Where relevant, the front and back of the folio is indicated by "a" or "b," respectively; and then the line number follows the slash mark. An example is BSP 21b/2.
2. See KKN ff. 26b/4.
3. See HSK 47.
4. JN ff. 4a/1–5a/2.
5. For the whole verse, please see DDG pp. 97/11.

Chapter 3: The Four Foundations of the Tulku Principle

1. Skt., *trikaya;* Tib., *sku gsum.*
2. KS ff. 56a/7.
3. YRD vol. E, ff. 42b/2.
4. Skt., *dharmakaya;* Tib., *ch'os sku.*
5. Skt., *sambhogakaya;* Tib., *longs sku.*
6. The five wisdoms are the five aspects of Buddha wisdom, as follows: (1) the Wisdom of the Ultimate Sphere—the purity of ignorance—is the aspect of the true nature of buddhahood that is openness (emptiness) and the changeless state free from elaboration, like space, where we attain total liberation; (2) the Mirrorlike Wisdom—the purity of hatred—facilitates the arising of the next three wisdoms, without subject-object duality, like the reflections arising in a mirror; (3) the Wisdom of Equanimity—the purity of arrogance—is the wisdom of realizing all in the oneness and evenness state, where there is no samsara or nirvana, good or bad; (4) the Distinguishing (or All-knowing) Wisdom—the purity of desire—is the wisdom that knows all the knowable fields, both as they are and in detail; (5) the Wisdom of Accomplishment—the purity of jealousy—is the wisdom that fulfills the needs of all spontaneously and effortlessly with various manifestations.
7. The five buddha-families are as follows: (a) the Buddha (Enlightenment) family, presided over by the union (oneness) of the male Buddha Vairocana (the purity of consciousness) and the female Buddha Dhatvisvari (the purity of space); (b) the Vajra (Adamantine) family, presided over by the union (oneness) of the male Aksobhya (or Vajrasattva) (the purity of form) and the female Buddha Locana (the purity of water); (c) the Ratna (Jewel) family, presided over by the union (oneness) of the male Buddha Ratnasambhava, the purity of feeling, and the female Buddha Mamaki, the purity of earth; (d) the Padma (Lotus) family, presided over by the union (oneness) of the male Buddha Amitabha (the purity of perception) and the female Buddha Pandaravasini (the purity of fire); (e) the Karma (Action) family, presided over by the union (oneness) of the male Buddha Amogasiddhi (the purity of formation) and the female Buddha Samayatara (the purity of air).
8. The Pure Land of the Enjoyment-body possesses the qualities of five certainties: (1) the place is self-appearing or self-present, free from dimensions; (2) the teachers are the Buddhas of the five classes

or families; (3) the disciples are infinite and inseparable from the teacher; (4) the teachings are great luminescent vision, ineffable beyond concepts or words; (5) the time is changeless and timeless time.

9. KJ 390/9 says, "They appear to the bodhisattvas of the first to the tenth stages."

10. Such as hatred, greed, jealousy, arrogance, and confusion.

11. Subjective and objective.

12. YSJ ff. 33a/7.

13. KJD 135/8 says, "There are four kinds of nirmanakaya: supreme, artisan, birth, and diverse manifestations."

14. DDG 47/6 says, "Always, buddhas appear in the forms of manifested-bodies of art, birth, and supreme beings for the sake of beings."

15. Skt., *uttama nirmanakaya;* Tib., *mch'og gi sprul sku.*

16. GB 26/17.

17. Skt., *shilpin nirmanakaya;* Tib., *bzo sprul sku.*

18. Skt., *janma nirmanakaya;* Tib., *skye ba sprul sku.*

19. Quoted a sutra in KZZ 309/16. "Final five-hundred-year period" means during the last five centuries of Buddhism, when followers will particularly need teachers.

20. Tib., *sna tshogs sprul sku.*

21. BSP ff. 21b/2.

22. BTT 32/1.

23. Skt., *bodhicitta;* Tib., *byang sems.*

24. Skt., *bodhisattva;* Tib. *byang ch'ub sems dpa'*

25. CND 31/15.

Chapter 4: The Three Main Types of Tulkus

1. Skt., *janma nirmanakaya;* Tib., *skye ba sprul sku.*

2. Tib., *ma 'das sprul sku.*

3. ML 78/12.

4. KBZ 340/8.

5. Based on KP ff. 1b/5.

6. According to mahayana philosophy, trainees advance to buddhahood through the five paths and ten stages. The five paths are the paths of accumulation, joining, seeing, meditation, and beyond training. The ten stages are the Joyous, the Stainless, the Radiant, the Brilliant, the Hard to Conquer, the Realized, the Far-reaching, the Unshakable,

the Good Intelligence, and the Cloud of Dharma. When you realize the path of seeing, you are attaining the first stage. During the path of meditation, you progress through the rest of the nine stages. The path of beyond training is buddhahood, and sometimes buddhahood is also called the eleventh stage as well as the All-radiant stage.

7. Skt., *siddha;* Tib., *grub thob.*
8. See KJ 369/17.
9. KJ 373/5: "The eleventh stage is called *'Kun tu od,'* and that is the path beyond training, the attainment of buddhahood."
10. TRG 309/9: "(They are) perfectly able to display a hundred physical manifestations, each with a retinue of a hundred bodhisattvas."
11. Tib., *mi shes pa'i rgyu bzhi.* See NG ff. 3b/7.
12. KBZ 257/12.
13. "Virtuous friend" is a common term in Indian and Tibetan Mahayana literature, meaning "spiritual guide." In Tibetan, *dGe ba'i bshes gnyen* (short version: *dGe bshes,* or *geshe.*) In Sanskrit, *kalyanamitra.*

Chapter 5: The Secondary Types of Tulkus

1. Tib., *ngos ma bzung pa'i sprul sku.*
2. See *Jatakamala* by Aryashura, which contains thirty-four life stories and *Kalpalata* by Ksemendra, which has 108 life stories. Their translation from Sanskrit into Tibetan can be found in the Kyerab section of the *Tenjur Collection.*
3. DSD ff. 117a/6.
4. A seeker of enlightenment for others.
5. Based on MNT ff. 3a/5.
6. Based on GTN.
7. See JSN ff. 4b/2.
8. Biography based on GSM ff.266/1.
9. MMM 118/1 and YN.
10. MMM 122/18.
11. JKS ff. 36/2.
12. The Fire Monkey year (1956) and the Fire Bird year (1957).
13. Tib., *byin gyis brlabs pa'i sprul sku.*
14. Tib., *byin gyis brlabs pa'i nus pa.*
15. See TNN ff. 9a/5.
16. MMM 283.

17. ML 78/14.
18. ML 78/23.
19. MMM 230.
20. Tib., *sprul log or sprul rgod.*
21. Tib., *rab byung.*
22. Tib., *sngags pa.*
23. TT ff. 118a/3.
24. GLS ff. 4a/1.
25. KZ 415/2.
26. DTC ff. 13a/3.
27. PT 476/15.
28. LA ff. 2a/4.
29. Skt., *sangha;* Tib., *dge 'dun.*
30. Tib., *dkor.*
31. Tib., *bsngo bsgyur.*
32. TPG ff. 251b/1.
33. KZ 571/10.
34. Tib., *sPrul rdzun.*
35. LKG 298/4.
36. NC 416/14.
37. DK p. 194/6.

Chapter 6: The Discovery and Recognition of Tulkus

1. NNG 31–32.
2. See ZS and LW. I heard the story of the palanquin from Tulku Dorje Dradul, the youngest son of Dudjom Lingpa.
3. Tib., *sbas yul.*
4. See LYN 344a/3.
5. Skt., *sukhavati;* Tib., *bde ba chan.* The name of Amitabha Buddha's pure land or paradise.
6. *Prajnaparamita.* In total there are fifteen volumes.
7. Tib., *Shes rab snying po.*
8. See HSK 127/11 and 129/16; and BS 59/5.
9. PDN 232/8 and ff. 245/5.
10. RDN ff. 4a/1.
11. HSK 55/8.
12. See BDT 99.1.
13. For *delog* (Tib., *'das log*), see PDJR 96–167.
14. See BDT 338/10.

15. MMM 181–82/10.

16. Tib., *Zangs mdog dpal ri*. It is the name of the pure land of Guru Padmasambhava.

17. See NB and MMM 251/1.

18. PLT ff. 4b/3.

19. Summarized from DKN 13–32.

20. DKN 8.

21. Based on BSK and KNT.

22. See MMM 298/1.

23. See KN, BM, MMM 292/1, and MGG 306/1.

24. See BM 288/32.

25. See BM 291/21.

26. See MMM 314/1 and MGG 326/36.

27. See MMM 324/18 and 326/15.

28. Tib., *sbas yul*.

29. See NW 153/13.

30. See MLP.

31. JKT 363/12.

32. Tib., *gter* or *gter ma*.

33. See HTT for detailed explanations of *ter* tradition.

34. Tib., *gter ston*.

35. Tib., *brda yig*.

36. Tib., *sa gter*; earth ter.

37. Tib., *dgongs gter*; mind ter.

38. See NTR 624–29:

39. Tib., *gNam ch'os*; "The Cycle of Space Treasures" is the collection of ter teachings practiced by the Palyul lineage of the Nyingma school.

40. Tib., *mtshan gsol rten 'brel* or *nab bza' gsol ba*.

41. Tib., *khri 'don rten 'brel*.

42. "*bzhengs shig padma 'byung gnas mkha' 'gro'i tshogs . . .*"

Chapter 7: Miraculous Deaths

1. *Ringsel* (Skt., *sarira*; Tib., *ring bsrel*), sacred relic. There are many kinds of ringsel, but the most significant ring-srels are the *ku dung* (*sku gdung*) ringsel—the ringsel produced from the ashes, the cremated bones, of fully enlightened masters, such as the Buddha himself. They are pellets, may look like pearls or white mustard seeds, and are hard and shiny. They can spontaneously multiply

or alternatively can vanish if they are kept improperly. They are mostly white, but the ringsel of most highly enlightened masters could also be in various colors. Ring-srels are the sacred gifts by the enlightened masters for their devotees as the objects of veneration and sources of blessings, instead of their dissolving as light. For detailed interpretations of different ringsel, see TRD, vol. Wam. ff. 192a/2.

2. Tib., *gsang sngags rnying ma,* or Nyingma; and *gsang sngags gsar ma,* or Sarma.

3. Tib., *'ja' lus.*

4. Tib., *Khregs ch'od.*

5. Tib., *Brag lha klu* is on the north side of Chagpori Hill.

6. DLT ff. 111b/2.

7. NPDN 130.

8. Tib., *'ja' lus 'pho ba ch'en po.*

9. Tib., *thod rgal.*

10. 60a/1, 68a/6, and see MMM pp. 68–73.

11. Tib., *sNying thig of rDzogs ch'en.*

12. This story is based on LYN 46a/6 and 78a/6. Also see MMM pp. 74–108.

13. Tib., *brdzus skyes.*

14. See LYN 109b/6.

15. Tib., *od lus su bzhengs.* See BMT 400. However, some say, it was rainbow body.

16. Kyala Khenpo explained this to me.

17. RBP ff. 104b/5.

18. See RBP ff. 20a/5, and MMM 92/33.

19. RBP ff. 99b/5.

20. See DD 110a/2.

21. Based on BMT 362/1 and other sources.

22. Tib., *bka' babs bdun.*

23. The following is a note jotted down by three students—Gunang Kitrug, Khenpo Jamdon, and Rekong Kulo, who were in his presence. But they could not catch or remember many of his explanations on the five wisdoms.

24. Sokhe Jomo was the name of a nun.

25. Tib., *Öd gsal,* clear light.

26. Tib., *yon tan rin ch'en rgyal po.*

27. Tib., *ma bchos chog bzhag.*

28. Tib., *sems nyid ngal gso.*

29. See LYN 314b4.
30. Tib., *bka' babs bdun.*
31. Tib., *Padmas khebs pa.*
32. Tib., *Padma'i myu gu.*
33. The following is based on the stories of eyewitnesses and on MGC 472/27.
34. Tib., *zhal chems* or *'das rjes zhal ch'ems.*
35. See KZ 156/2. Also see MMM 158/15 and 190/34.
36. Based on LLP, vol. 1, pp. 930/4.
37. Tib., *snyan rgyud* or *dga' ldan snyan rgyud.*
38. Tib., *ma dag pa'i sgyu lus.*
39. Tib., *'ja lus rdo rje'i sku.*
40. See DN, vol 1, pp. 94/13; and KG, vol. 1, pp. 627/7.
41. MN 169/21.
42. Tib., *mNgon dga'i zhing du bchom ldan 'das Mi bskyod pa.*
43. See NGN and GSM 129/3.
44. Tib., *lam rim.*
45. GSM pp. 211/3 GS ff.5b/2
46. Tib., *lam 'bras.*
47. GSM 201/3; KG, vol. 2, pp. 1366/4; and GS ff. 14b2.
48. SN ff. 67a/3.
49. GSM 266/2 and LLP, vol. 1, 649/4.
50. Tib., *sku 'bum.*
51. Tib., *seng ge'i nga ro;* Skt., *sinhanada.* Based on LLP, vol. 1, pp. 649/4, and GSM 266/2.
52. AFP 400/3.
53. See BT 26/15 and CT 503/30.
54. DN, vol. 1, pp. 564/3, and HSK.
55. DN, vol. 2, pp. 779/17, and GSM.
56. SN ff. 216b/1 and DR 66/10.
57. See KSN.
58. DN, vol 2, pp. 702/1.
59. DN, vol 2, pp. 717/9.
60. TLP 383/2.

Chapter 8: Miracles of Adepts versus Paranormal Events

1. Skt., *asura;* Tib., *lha ma yin.*
2. The god, demigod, human, animal, hungry ghost, and hell realms.
3. St., *bumipati;* Tib., *yul lha* or *gzhi bdag.*

4. Skt., *dharmapala;* Tib., *ch'os skyong.*
5. MK 48/12.
6. MK 71/4.
7. This story is based on what I heard from my mother, who learned it from her father.
8. Tib., *bsang;* incense offering.
9. Tib., *sman mo.*
10. Tib., *glud* or *glud bsngo ba.*
11. See KG, vol 1, pp. 526/22.
12. A class of beings believed to reside mostly in lakes, rivers, or underground.

Chapter 9: Common Questions

1. See MGG 216/4 and MMM 163/1.
2. See MMM 314.
3. See MMM 298.
4. They are Chökyi Wangpo (1894–1909) of Dzongsar, Chökyi Lodrö (1893–1959) of Kathok (he later became the Dzongsar Khyentse), Karma Khyentse Ozer (1896–1945) of Palpung (Beri), Guru Tsewang (1897–?) of Dzogchen, Kunzang Drodul Dechen Dorje (1897—1946) of Dza Palme, and Dilgo Khyentse Tashi Paljor (1910–91) of Zhechen.
5. DSR ff. 46b/3.
6. DDG 97/11.
7. Being from a nomadic background, Paltrul Rinpoche illustrates his teachings with some imagery of the nomadic culture of wild Eastern Tibet.
8. See GNT ff. 2b/2.
9. Skt., *vinaya;* Tib., *'dul ba.*
10. BP ff. 110a/4.
11. A kind of mystical bird.

Chapter 10: How to Become and Function as a Tulku

1. Skt., *maitri;* Tib., *byams pa.* For detailed meditations on loving-kindness, please read HPLK.
2. Skt., *Avalokitesvara;* Tib., *spyan ras gzigs.*
3. MRN ff. 184b/6.
4. TT ff. 289b/3.

5. The two form-bodies of the Buddha are the enjoyment-body and the manifested-body.

6. GTR 95/3.

7. CND 77/15.

8. Skt., *samgraha-vastu;* Tib., *bsdu ba'i dngos po.* See BLC 462/2.

9. See BLC 462/5.

10. See TGS ff. 67a/5.

11. BP ff. 137a/5.

CREDITS

Page 6. The Second Karmapa. Illustrated by Namkha Tashi. From *The History of the Sixteen Karmapas of Tibet.* Reprinted with permission from Shambhala Publications, Inc., Boston, Mass. www .shambhala.com.

Page 8. The Second Dalai Lama. Illustrated by Chris Banigan. From *The Second Dalai Lama: His Life and Teachings.* Reprinted courtesy of Snow Lion Publications. PO Box 6483, Ithaca, NY 14851. www.snowlion pub.com.

Page 29. Je Tsongkhapa. Illustrated by Robert Beer. From *The Tibet Guide: Central and Western Tibet.* Reprinted courtesy of Wisdom Publications, 199 Elm Street, Somerville, MA 02114. www .wisdompubs.org.

Page 30. Rigdzin Jigme Lingpa. Photographer unknown. From the collection of Choten Gonpa.

Page 48. Kyabje Dudjom Rinpoche. Photograph by James George. From the collection of Tulku Thondup.

Page 49. Sakya Trizin. Photographer unknown. From the collection of Sakya Trizin.

Page 51. The Sixteenth Karmapa. Photographer unknown. From the collection of the Shambhala Archives.

Page 54. Do Khyentse Yeshe Dorje. From the collection of Choten Gonpa.

Page 56. Shugseb Lochen Chönyi Zangmo. From the collection of Tsewang Namtrol.

Page 57. Khenpo Ngagchung. Photographer unknown. From the collection of Tulku Thondup.

Page 61. Sera Khandro. Photograph by Sarah Jacoby. From the collection of Tralag Khenpo.

Page 63. Rigdzin Tenpe Gyaltsen. Photographer unknown. From the collection of Tulku Thondup.

Page 64. Dilgo Khyentse Rinpoche. Photograph by Matthieu Ricard. From the collection of Matthieu Ricard.

Page 65. Khyentse Yangsi Rinpoche. Photograph by Matthieu Ricard. From the collection of Matthieu Ricard.

Page 67. The Fourth Dodrupchen Rinpoche. Photographer unknown. From the collection of Tulku Thondup.

Page 68. Pema Norbu Rinpoche. Photographer unknown. From the collection of the Shambhala Archives.

Page 69. The Fifth Dzogchen Rinpoche. Photographer unknown. From the collection of Tulku Thondup.

Page 70. The Fourteenth Dalai Lama. Photograph by Brian Beresford. From the collection of Brian Beresford.

Page 79. Padma Duddul. Illustrator unknown. From the collection of Rigpa International.

Page 79. Padma Duddul's hair. Photograph by Jim Rosen. From the collection of Tulku Thondup.

Page 80. Sonam Namgyal's mole hair and nail. Photograph by Jim Rosen. From the collection of Tulku Thondup.

Page 82. Guru Padmasambhava: Meditation support of the Second Dodrupchen, Lushul Khenpo, and Kyala Khenpo. Photograph by Jim Rosen. From the collection of Tulku Thondup.

Page 84. Ringsels of Kunkhen Longchen Rabjam (left) and of Dharma Senge (right). Photograph by Jim Rosen. From the collection of Tulku Thondup.

Page 86. Jamyang Khyentse'i Wangpo. Reprinted from *nNying ma'i ch'os 'byung* by Kyabje Dudjom Rinpoche.

Page 91. Khenpo Tsewang Rigdzin. Photographer unknown. From the collection of Tulku Thondup.

Page 96. Milarepa. Illustration by Robert Beer. From *The Tibet Guide: Central and Western Tibet*. Reprinted courtesy of Wisdom Publications, 199 Elm Street, Somerville, MA 02114. www.wisdompubs.org.

Page 101. Chögyam Trungpa Rinpoche in Japan. Photograph by Andrea Roth. Reprinted by permission from the collection of Andrea Roth.

INDEX

ABOUT THE AUTHOR

TULKU THONDUP RINPOCHE is a prolific writer born in Golok in Eastern Tibet. At the age of four he was recognized as a tulku and studied at the famed Dodrupchen Monastery. He moved to India in 1958 and taught at Lucknow University (1967–76) and Visva Bharati University (1976–80). He came to the United States as a Visiting Scholar at Harvard University (1980–83). He has authored and translated about a dozen books on Tibetan Buddhism under the auspices of the Buddhayana Foundation, an organization dedicated to preserving Tibetan Buddhism. He travels throughout North America, Europe, and Asia to give talks on Buddhism and lead meditation workshops. For the last thirty years, he has lived in Cambridge, Massachusetts.

Printed in the United States
By Bookmasters